# bowl
# food

# bowl
# food

LAUREL
GLEN
San Diego, California

# Contents

Soups 6

Salads 70

Pasta 126

Rice 190

Wok 232

Curries 290

One pots 342

Index 394

# Soups

## Spicy squash and coconut soup

1 small fresh red chili, seeded
  and chopped
1 lemongrass stalk, white part only,
  sliced
1 teaspoon ground cilantro
1 tablespoon chopped fresh ginger
2 cups vegetable stock
2 tablespoons vegetable oil
1 onion, finely chopped
1 3/4 lbs. squash flesh, cubed
  (see Note)
1 1/2 cups coconut milk
3 tablespoons chopped fresh
  cilantro leaves
2 teaspoons light brown sugar
extra cilantro leaves, to garnish

Process the chili, lemongrass, ground cilantro, ginger, and 2 tablespoons vegetable stock in a food processor to form a smooth paste.

Heat the oil in a large saucepan, add the onion, and cook over medium heat for 5 minutes. Add the spice paste and cook, stirring, for 1 minute.

Add the squash and remaining vegetable stock. Bring to a boil, then reduce the heat and simmer, covered, for 15–20 minutes or until the squash is tender. Cool slightly, then process in a food processor or blender until smooth. Return to the cleaned saucepan, stir in the coconut milk, cilantro, and brown sugar, and simmer until hot. Garnish with the extra cilantro leaves.

Serves 4

Note: You will need to buy 3 lbs. of squash to yield 1 3/4 lbs. of flesh.

# Miso soup with chicken and udon noodles

8 dried shiitake mushrooms
1 1/4 lbs. skinless, boneless chicken
   breasts, cut into 1/2-inch-thick strips
1/4 cup white miso paste
2 teaspoons dashi granules
1 tablespoon wakame flakes or other
   seaweed (see Note)
3/4 lb. baby bok choy, halved
   lengthwise
3/4 lb. fresh udon noodles
5 oz. silken firm tofu, cut into
   1/2-inch cubes
3 scallions, sliced diagonally

Soak the mushrooms in 1 cup boiling water for 20 minutes. Drain, setting aside the liquid; discard the stems and thinly slice the caps.

Pour 8 cups water into a saucepan and bring to a boil, then reduce the heat and simmer. Add the chicken and cook for 2–3 minutes or until almost cooked through.

Add the mushrooms and cook for 1 minute, then add the miso paste, dashi granules, wakame, and mushroom liquid. Stir to dissolve the dashi and miso paste. Do not boil.

Add the bok choy halves and simmer for 1 minute or until beginning to wilt, then add the noodles and simmer for another 2 minutes. Gently stir in the tofu and ladle the hot soup into large serving bowls. Garnish with the sliced scallions.

Serves 4–6

Note: Wakame is a curly leafed, brown algae with a mild vegetable taste and a soft texture. It can be used in salads or can be boiled and served like a vegetable. Use a small amount, as it swells by about ten times after being cooked.

# Tomato bread soup

1½ lbs. vine-ripened tomatoes
1 loaf (1 lb.) day-old crusty Italian
 bread
1 tablespoon olive oil
3 cloves garlic, crushed
1 tablespoon tomato paste
5 cups hot vegetable stock
4 tablespoons torn fresh basil leaves
2–3 tablespoons extra-virgin olive oil
extra-virgin olive oil, to serve

Score a cross in the bottom of each tomato. Place in a bowl of boiling water for 1 minute, then plunge into cold water and peel the skin away from the cross. Cut the tomatoes in half and scoop out the seeds with a spoon. Chop the tomato flesh.

Remove most of the crust from the bread and discard. Cut the bread into 1-inch pieces.

Heat the oil in a large saucepan. Add the garlic, tomatoes, and tomato paste, then reduce the heat and simmer, stirring occasionally, for 10–15 minutes or until reduced and thickened. Add the stock and bring to a boil, stirring for 2–3 minutes. Reduce the heat to medium, add the bread pieces, and cook, stirring, for 5 minutes or until the bread softens and absorbs most of the liquid. Add more stock or water if necessary.

Stir in the torn basil leaves and extra-virgin olive oil, and allow to rest for 5 minutes so the flavors have time to develop. Drizzle with a little extra-virgin olive oil.

Serves 4

# Five-spice duck and somen noodle soup

4 duck breasts, skin left on
1 teaspoon five-spice powder
1 teaspoon peanut oil
7 oz. dried somen noodles

*Star anise broth*
4 cups chicken stock
3 whole star anise
5 scallions, chopped
1/4 cup chopped fresh cilantro leaves

Preheat the oven to 400°F. Trim the duck breasts of excess fat, then lightly sprinkle both sides with the five-spice powder.

Heat the oil in a large frying pan. Add the duck skin-side down and cook over medium heat for 2–3 minutes or until brown and crisp. Turn and cook the other side for 3 minutes. Transfer to a baking tray and cook, skin-side up, for another 8–10 minutes or until cooked through.

Meanwhile, place the chicken stock and star anise in a small saucepan. Bring to a boil, then reduce the heat and simmer for 5 minutes. Add the scallions and cilantro and simmer for 5 minutes.

Cook the noodles in a saucepan of boiling water for 2 minutes or until soft. Drain and divide among 4 bowls. Ladle the broth on the noodles and top each bowl with a sliced duck breast.

Serves 4

# Beef and beet borscht

2 tablespoons olive oil
1 onion, chopped
2 cloves garlic, crushed
1 lb. beef chuck, cut into 1-inch
  cubes
4 cups beef stock
2 small beets (½ lb.)
7 oz. canned crushed tomatoes
1 carrot, diced
½ lb. potatoes, diced
2½ cups finely shredded cabbage
2 teaspoons lemon juice
2 teaspoons sugar
2 tablespoons chopped fresh
  Italian parsley
2 tablespoons chopped fresh dill
⅓ cup sour cream

Preheat the oven to 400°F. Heat the oil in a large saucepan and cook the onion and garlic over medium heat for 3–5 minutes. Add the beef, stock, and 4 cups water, and bring to a boil. Reduce the heat and simmer, covered, for 1 hour, 15 minutes or until the meat is tender. Remove the meat.

Trim the beets just above the end of the leaf stems. Wrap in aluminum foil and bake for 30–40 minutes or until tender. Remove foil and allow to cool.

Return the stock to a boil and add the tomatoes, carrot, and potatoes, and season with salt. Cook over medium heat for 10 minutes. Add the cabbage and cook for 5 minutes. Peel and dice the beets. Return the meat to the saucepan and add the beets, lemon juice, sugar, and 1½ tablespoons each of parsley and dill. Cook for 2 minutes or until heated through. Season to taste.

Remove from the heat and allow to rest for 10 minutes. Serve with a dollop of sour cream and garnish with the remaining dill and parsley.

Serves 4

# Shrimp laksa

1 1/2 tablespoons cilantro seeds
1 tablespoon cumin seeds
1 teaspoon ground turmeric
1 onion, roughly chopped
1/2 x 1 1/4-inch piece fresh ginger,
  peeled and roughly chopped
3 cloves garlic
3 lemongrass stalks, white part
  only, sliced
6 macadamia nuts
4–6 small fresh red chilies
2–3 teaspoons shrimp paste
4 cups chicken stock
1/4 cup vegetable oil
3 cups coconut milk
4 fresh kaffir lime leaves
2 1/2 tablespoons lime juice
2 tablespoons fish sauce
2 tablespoons light brown sugar
1 1/2 lbs. raw medium shrimp, peeled
  and deveined, with tails intact
1/2 lb. dried rice vermicelli noodles
1 cup bean sprouts
4 fried tofu puffs, julienned
3 tablespoons roughly chopped
  fresh Vietnamese mint
2/3 cup fresh cilantro leaves
lime wedges, to serve

Roast the cilantro seeds over medium heat for 1–2 minutes or until fragrant, tossing constantly to prevent burning. Grind in a mortar and pestle or spice grinder. Repeat with the cumin seeds. Place all of the spices, onion, ginger, garlic, lemongrass, macadamias, chilies, and shrimp paste in a blender, add 1/2 cup stock, and blend to a paste.

Heat the oil over low heat and cook the paste for 3–5 minutes, stirring constantly to prevent it from burning or sticking. Add the remaining stock, bring to a boil, then reduce the heat and simmer for 15 minutes or until reduced slightly. Add the coconut milk, lime leaves, lime juice, fish sauce, and brown sugar, and simmer for 5 minutes. Add the shrimp and simmer for 2 minutes or until they are pink and cooked through. Do not boil or cover.

Soak the vermicelli in boiling water for 5 minutes or until soft. Drain and divide among serving bowls with most of the sprouts. Ladle hot soup over the noodles and garnish each bowl with tofu, mint, cilantro leaves, and the remaining bean sprouts. Serve with lime wedges.

Serves 4–6

## Caramelized onion and parsnip soup

2 tablespoons butter
3 large onions, halved and thinly sliced
2 tablespoons firmly packed light brown sugar
1 cup dry white wine
3 large parsnips, peeled and chopped
5 cups vegetable stock
1/4 cup cream
fresh thyme leaves, to garnish

Melt the butter in a large saucepan. Add the onions and sugar and cook over low heat for 10 minutes. Add the wine and parsnips and simmer, covered, for 20 minutes or until the onions and parsnips are golden and tender.

Pour in the stock, bring to a boil, then reduce the heat and simmer, covered, for 10 minutes. Cool slightly, then place in a blender or food processor and blend in batches until smooth. Season. Drizzle with a little cream and sprinkle fresh thyme leaves over the top. Serve with toasted crusty bread slices.

Serves 4

# Thai-style chicken and coconut soup

2 lemongrass stalks, white part finely chopped, tops set aside and halved
6 cloves garlic, chopped
3 red Asian shallots, chopped
8 black peppercorns
1 teaspoon store-bought red curry paste
1 cup coconut cream
1²/₃ cups coconut milk
1²/₃ cups chicken stock
2½ tablespoons thinly sliced fresh galangal
7 kaffir lime leaves, shredded
³/₄ lb. skinned, boneless chicken breasts or thighs, thinly sliced
2 tablespoons lime juice
2 tablespoons fish sauce
1 teaspoon light brown sugar
3 tablespoons fresh cilantro leaves
1 small fresh red chili, thinly sliced

Process the chopped lemongrass, garlic, shallots, peppercorns, and curry paste in a food processor to form a paste.

Heat a wok over low heat, add the coconut cream, increase the heat to high, and bring to a boil. Add the paste and cook, stirring, for 5 minutes. Add the coconut milk and stock, return to a boil, and add the sliced galangal, the kaffir lime leaves, and the remaining lemongrass stalks. Reduce the heat and simmer for 5 minutes.

Add the chicken and simmer for 8 minutes or until cooked. Stir in the lime juice, fish sauce, brown sugar, cilantro leaves, and chili. Serve immediately.

Serves 4

# Rice noodle soup with duck

1 whole roast duck
4 fresh cilantro roots and stems,
   well rinsed
5 slices fresh galangal
4 scallions, sliced diagonally into
   1-inch pieces
3/4 lb. Chinese kale, cut into
   2-inch pieces
2 cloves garlic, crushed
3 tablespoons fish sauce
1 tablespoon hoisin sauce
2 teaspoons light brown sugar
1/2 teaspoon ground white pepper
1 lb. fresh rice noodles
crispy fried garlic flakes, to garnish
   (optional)
fresh cilantro leaves, to garnish
   (optional)

To make the stock, cut off the duck's head with a sharp knife and discard. Remove the skin and fat, leaving the neck intact. Carefully remove the flesh from the bones and set aside. Cut any visible fat from the carcass along with the tailpiece, then discard. Break the carcass into large pieces, then place in a large stockpot with 8 cups water.

Lightly smash the cilantro roots and stems with the back of a knife. Add to the pot with the galangal and bring to a boil. Skim off any impurities from the surface. Boil over medium heat for 15 minutes. Strain the stock through a fine strainer, discard the carcass, and return the stock to a clean saucepan.

Slice the duck flesh into strips. Add to the stock with the scallions, Chinese kale, garlic, fish sauce, hoisin sauce, brown sugar, and white pepper. Gently bring to a boil.

Cook the noodles in boiling water for 2–3 minutes or until tender. Drain well. Divide the noodles and soup evenly among the serving bowls. If desired, garnish with the garlic flakes and cilantro leaves. Serve immediately.

Serves 4–6

# Hearty bean and pasta soup

1 tablespoon olive oil
1 onion, finely chopped
3 cloves garlic, crushed
10-oz. can cannellini beans, drained
10-oz. can kidney beans, drained
7 cups chicken stock (see Note)
3 oz. conchigliette pasta
1 tablespoon chopped fresh tarragon

Heat the oil in a saucepan over low heat. Add the onion and cook for 5 minutes, then add the garlic and cook for another minute, stirring frequently. Add the beans and chicken stock, cover the saucepan with a lid, and bring to a boil. Add the pasta and cook until al dente. Stir in the tarragon, then season with salt and black pepper. Serve with crusty bread.

Serves 4

Note: The flavor of this soup is enhanced by using a good-quality stock.

# Shrimp, potato, and corn chowder

1 1/4 lbs. medium shrimp
3 corncobs, husks and silks removed
1 tablespoon olive oil
2 leeks, white part only, finely
  chopped
2 cloves garlic, crushed
1 1/4 lbs. potatoes, cut into
  1/2-inch cubes
3 cups fish or chicken stock
1 1/2 cups milk
1 cup cream
pinch of cayenne pepper
3 tablespoons finely chopped fresh
  Italian parsley

Peel and devein the shrimp, then chop into 1/2-inch pieces.

Cut the kernels from the corncobs. Heat the oil in a large saucepan and add the leeks. Cook over medium-low heat for 5 minutes or until soft and lightly golden. Add the garlic and cook for 30 seconds, then add the corn, potatoes, stock, and milk.

Bring to a boil, then reduce the heat and simmer, partially covered, for 20 minutes or until the potatoes are soft but still hold their shape (they will break down slightly). Remove the lid and simmer for another 10 minutes to allow the soup to thicken. Reduce the heat to low. Put 2 cups of the soup in a blender and blend until very smooth.

Return the blended soup to the saucepan and add the shrimp. Increase the heat to medium and simmer for 2 minutes or until the shrimp are pink and cooked through. Stir in the cream, cayenne pepper, and 2 tablespoons of the parsley. Season to taste with salt, then serve garnished with the remaining parsley.

Serves 4–6

# Pea and arugula soup

1 tablespoon olive oil
1 red onion, finely chopped
1 1/2 lbs. frozen peas
3 cups arugula leaves
3 cups hot vegetable stock
shaved Parmesan, to garnish
extra arugula leaves, to garnish

Heat the oil in a large saucepan over medium heat. Add the onion and cook for 5 minutes or until soft. Add the peas and arugula and cook for another 2 minutes. Add the stock and 1 cup water, bring to a boil, then reduce the heat and simmer for 20 minutes.

Cool slightly, then place in a food processor or blender in batches and process until almost smooth. Return to the cleaned saucepan and heat through. Serve garnished with shaved Parmesan and the extra arugula.

Serves 4

# Vegetable ramen

3/4 lb. fresh ramen noodles
1 tablespoon vegetable oil
1 tablespoon finely chopped fresh
  ginger
2 cloves garlic, crushed
1 2/3 cups oyster mushrooms, halved
1 small zucchini, sliced into thin
  rounds
1 leek, white and light green parts,
  halved lengthwise and thinly sliced
1/4 lb. snow peas, halved diagonally
1/4 lb. fried tofu puffs, cut into
  matchsticks
5 cups vegetable stock
1 1/2 tablespoons white miso paste
2 tablespoons light soy sauce
1 tablespoon mirin
1 cup bean sprouts
1 teaspoon sesame oil
4 scallions, thinly sliced
1 cup enoki mushrooms

Bring a large saucepan of lightly salted water to a boil. Add the noodles and cook, stirring to keep them from sticking, for 4 minutes or until just tender. Drain and rinse under cold running water.

Heat the oil in a large saucepan over medium heat, then add the ginger, crushed garlic, oyster mushrooms, zucchini, leek, snow peas, and tofu puffs, and stir-fry for 2 minutes. Add the stock and 1 1/4 cups water and bring to a boil, then reduce the heat and simmer. Stir in the miso, soy sauce, and mirin until heated through. Do not boil. Stir in the bean sprouts and sesame oil.

Place the noodles in the bottom of 6 serving bowls, then pour in the soup. Garnish with the scallions and enoki mushrooms.

Serves 6

# Chicken and squash laksa

*Paste*
2 bird's-eye chilies, seeded and
  roughly chopped
2 lemongrass stalks, white part only,
  roughly chopped
4 red Asian shallots, peeled
1 tablespoon roughly chopped fresh
  ginger
1 teaspoon ground turmeric
3 candlenuts or macadamia nuts
  (optional)

1/4 lb. dried rice noodle sticks
1 tablespoon peanut oil
1/2 lb. butternut squash, cut into
  3/4-inch chunks
3 cups coconut milk
1 1/4 lbs. skinless, boneless chicken
  breasts, cut into cubes
2 tablespoons lime juice
1 tablespoon fish sauce
1 cup bean sprouts
1/2 cup torn fresh basil
1/2 cup torn fresh mint
1/2 cup unsalted peanuts, roasted
  and chopped
1 lime, cut into quarters

Place all the paste ingredients in a food processor with 1 tablespoon water and blend until smooth.

Soak the noodles in boiling water for 15–20 minutes. Drain.

Meanwhile, heat the oil in a wok and swirl to coat. Add the paste and stir over low heat for 5 minutes or until aromatic. Add the squash and coconut milk and simmer for 10 minutes. Add the chicken and simmer for 20 minutes. Stir in the lime juice and fish sauce.

Divide the noodles among 4 deep serving bowls, then ladle the soup over them. Garnish with the bean sprouts, basil, mint, peanuts, and lime wedges.

Serves 4

# Chickpea soup

1 1/2 cups dried chickpeas
1/2 brown onion
1 bay leaf
8 cloves garlic, unpeeled
2 tablespoons olive oil
1 celery stalk, chopped
1 large yellow onion, finely chopped
3 cloves garlic, chopped
1 teaspoon ground cumin
1 teaspoon paprika
1/4 teaspoon dried chili powder
3 teaspoons chopped fresh oregano
4 cups vegetable stock
2 tablespoons lemon juice
olive oil, to drizzle

Place the chickpeas in a bowl and cover with water. Soak overnight, then drain. Transfer to a saucepan and add the brown onion, bay leaf, 8 garlic cloves, and 5 cups water. Bring to a boil, then reduce the heat and simmer for 1 hour or until the chickpeas are tender. Drain, saving 2 cups of cooking liquid. Discard the onion, bay leaf, and garlic cloves.

Heat the oil in a saucepan, add the celery and chopped yellow onion, and cook over medium heat for 5 minutes or until golden. Add the chopped garlic and cook for another minute. Add the cumin, paprika, chili powder, and 2 teaspoons of the oregano, and cook, stirring, for 1 minute. Return the chickpeas to the saucepan and stir to coat with the spices.

Pour in the vegetable stock and cooking liquid, bring to a boil, then reduce the heat and simmer for 20 minutes. Stir in the lemon juice and remaining oregano and serve drizzled with olive oil.

Serves 4

# Crab and corn eggflower noodle broth

3 oz. dried, thin egg noodles
1 tablespoon peanut oil
1 teaspoon finely chopped fresh
   ginger
3 scallions, thinly sliced, white
   and green parts separated
5 cups chicken stock
1/3 cup mirin
1/2 lb. baby corn, sliced diagonally
   into 1/2-inch slices
6 oz. fresh crabmeat
1 tablespoon cornstarch, mixed
   with 1 tablespoon water
2 eggs, lightly beaten
2 teaspoons lime juice
1 tablespoon soy sauce
1/4 cup torn fresh cilantro leaves

Cook the noodles in boiling salted water for 3 minutes or until just tender. Drain and rinse under cold water.

Heat the oil in a large, heavy-bottomed saucepan. Add the ginger and the scallions (white part) and cook over medium heat for 1–2 minutes. Add the stock, mirin, and corn, and bring to a boil. Simmer for about 5 minutes. Stir in the noodles, crabmeat, and the cornstarch mixture. Return to a simmer, stirring constantly until it thickens. Reduce the heat and pour in the egg in a thin stream, stirring constantly—do not boil. Gently stir in the lime juice, soy sauce, and half the cilantro.

Divide the noodles among 4 bowls and ladle the soup on top. Garnish with the scallions (green part) and cilantro leaves.

Serves 4

# Hot and sour shrimp soup

3/4 lb. medium shrimp
1 tablespoon vegetable oil
3 lemongrass stalks, white part only
3 thin slices fresh galangal
3–5 small fresh red chilies
5 fresh kaffir lime leaves, finely
    shredded
2 tablespoons fish sauce
2 scallions, sliced
1/2 cup canned straw mushrooms,
    drained, or quartered button
    mushrooms
3 tablespoons lime juice
1–2 tablespoons chili paste,
    or to taste
fresh cilantro leaves, to garnish
    (optional)

Peel and devein the shrimp, leaving the tail intact and saving the heads and shells. Heat the oil in a large stockpot or wok and add the shrimp heads and shells. Cook for 5 minutes or until the shells turn bright orange. Lightly smash 1 lemongrass stalk with the back of a knife. Add to the pot with the galangal and 8 cups water. Bring to a boil, then reduce the heat and simmer for 20 minutes. Strain the stock and return to the pot. Discard the shells and herbs.

Finely slice the chilies and remaining lemongrass. Add to the liquid with the lime leaves, fish sauce, scallions, and mushrooms. Cook gently for 2 minutes.

Add the shrimp and cook for 3 minutes or until the shrimp are tender. Add the lime juice and chili paste (adjust to taste with extra lime juice or fish sauce). If desired, garnish with cilantro leaves.

Serves 4–6

Notes: To add more flavor and depth, replace the water with chicken stock. Chili paste with soybean oil is sometimes called "chili jam" and is available from Asian food stores.

## Sweet potato and pear soup

1 tablespoon butter
1 small white onion, finely chopped
1½ lbs. orange sweet potatoes,
   peeled and cut into ¾-inch dice
2 firm pears, peeled, cored, and cut
   into ¾-inch dice
3 cups chicken or vegetable stock
1 cup whipping cream
chopped fresh mint, to garnish

Melt the butter in a saucepan over medium heat, add the onion, and cook for 2–3 minutes or until softened but not brown. Add the sweet potatoes and pears and cook, stirring, for 1–2 minutes. Add the stock to the saucepan, bring to a boil, and cook for 20 minutes or until the sweet potatoes and pears are soft.

Cool slightly, then place the mixture in a blender or food processor and blend in batches until smooth. Return to the saucepan, stir in the cream, and gently reheat without boiling. Season with salt and ground black pepper. Garnish with the fresh mint.

Serves 4

Note: This soup can be frozen before you add the cream. To serve, defrost the soup, then gently reheat, stirring in the cream.

# Beef pho

6 oz. rice noodle sticks
6 cups beef stock
1 star anise
1 1/2-inch piece fresh ginger, sliced
2 pig's feet (ask your butcher
  to cut them in half)
1/2 onion, studded with 2 cloves
2 lemongrass stalks, pounded
2 cloves garlic, pounded
1/4 teaspoon white pepper
1 tablespoon fish sauce
3/4-lb. fillet of beef, partially frozen
  and thinly sliced
1 cup bean sprouts
2 scallions, thinly sliced diagonally
1/2 cup fresh cilantro leaves, chopped
1/2 cup fresh Vietnamese mint,
  chopped
1 fresh red chili, thinly sliced
fresh red chilies, to serve
fresh Vietnamese mint, to serve
fresh cilantro leaves, to serve
2 limes, cut into quarters
fish sauce, to serve

Soak the noodles in boiling water for 15–20 minutes. Drain.

Bring the stock, star anise, ginger, pig's feet, onion, lemongrass, garlic, and white pepper to a boil in a large saucepan. Reduce the heat and simmer for 30 minutes. Strain, return to the same saucepan, and stir in the fish sauce.

Divide the noodles among bowls, then top with beef strips, sprouts, scallions, cilantro, mint, and chili slices. Ladle on the broth.

Place the extra chilies, mint, cilantro, lime quarters, and fish sauce in small bowls on a platter, serve with the soup, and allow your guests to help themselves.

Serves 4

# Corn and lemongrass soup with crayfish

4 corncobs
1 tablespoon vegetable oil
1 leek, white part only, chopped
1 celery stick, chopped
3 lemongrass stalks, white part
  only, lightly smashed
2 cloves garlic, crushed
1 teaspoon ground cumin
1 teaspoon ground cilantro
3/4 teaspoon ground white pepper
3 kaffir lime leaves
3 cups chicken stock
3 1/4 cups coconut milk
1/2 cup cream
2 teaspoons butter
3 cloves garlic, crushed
1/2 teaspoon sambal oelek
2 1/2 lbs. cooked crayfish or jumbo
  shrimp, meat removed and
  shredded
1 tablespoon finely chopped fresh
  cilantro leaves

Trim the kernels from the corn. Heat the oil over medium heat, add the leek, celery, and lemongrass, and stir for 10 minutes or until the leek is soft. Add the garlic, cumin, cilantro, and 1/2 teaspoon of the pepper and cook, stirring, for 1–2 minutes or until fragrant. Add the corn, lime leaves, stock, and coconut milk, stir well, and simmer, stirring occasionally, for 1 1/2 hours. Remove from the heat and cool slightly. Remove the lemongrass and lime leaves and blend the mixture in batches in a food processor until smooth.

Push the mixture through a strainer with a wooden spoon. Repeat. Return to a large, clean saucepan, add the cream, and warm gently.

Melt the butter in a frying pan over medium heat, add the extra garlic, sambal oelek, remaining pepper, and a pinch of salt, and stir for 1 minute. Add the crayfish meat, stir for another minute or until heated through, then remove from the heat and stir in the fresh cilantro.

Ladle the soup into shallow soup bowls, then pile some crayfish meat in the center of each bowl.

Serves 4 (6 as an appetizer)

## Green tea noodle soup

½ lb. dried green tea noodles
2 teaspoons dashi granules
1 tablespoon mirin
1 tablespoon Japanese soy sauce
½ lb. firm tofu, drained and cut into
   ½-inch cubes
1 sheet nori, shredded
3 teaspoons roasted sesame seeds

Cook the noodles in a large saucepan of boiling salted water for 5 minutes or until tender. Drain and rinse under cold water.

Combine the dashi granules with 6 cups water in a large saucepan. Stir over medium-high heat until the granules are dissolved. Increase the heat to high and bring to a boil. Stir in the mirin and soy sauce.

Divide the noodles and tofu cubes among 4 serving bowls and ladle the hot stock on top. Garnish with the nori and sesame seeds. Serve immediately.

Serves 4

# Minestrone

2 cups dried cannellini or borlotti
  beans
1 tablespoon olive oil
3 oz. mild pancetta, finely diced
1 onion, chopped
1 carrot, diced
2 celery stalks, diced
1 large potato, diced
2 cloves garlic, crushed
3 tablespoons tomato paste
2 14-oz. cans crushed tomatoes
3 cups beef stock
1 cup elbow macaroni or ditalini
1 cup shredded cabbage
2 tablespoons shredded fresh basil
shaved Parmesan, to serve
extra-virgin olive oil, to serve

Place the beans in a large bowl, cover with cold water, and allow to soak overnight.

Heat the oil in a large saucepan, add the pancetta, and cook over medium heat, stirring, for 1–2 minutes or until slightly crisp. Add the onion, carrot, celery, potato, and garlic, and cook for 1–2 minutes. Add the tomato paste, tomatoes, beef stock, and drained beans. Bring to a boil, then reduce the heat and simmer, covered, for 40 minutes or until the beans are tender. (Do not add salt prior to this stage, as it will toughen the beans.)

Add the pasta and cabbage and cook for another 15 minutes. Season with salt and black pepper. Serve in deep bowls with the basil, shaved Parmesan, a drizzle of extra-virgin olive oil, and wood-fired bread.

Serves 6

# Sukiyaki soup

1/4 oz. dried sliced shiitake
  mushrooms
1/4 lb. dried rice vermicelli
2 teaspoons vegetable oil
1 leek, halved and sliced
4 cups chicken stock
1 teaspoon dashi granules, dissolved
  in 2 cups boiling water
1/2 cup soy sauce
2 tablespoons mirin
1 1/2 tablespoons sugar
2 cups shredded Chinese cabbage
  (wom buk)
10 oz. silken, firm tofu, cut into
  1-inch cubes
1 1/4 lbs. beef rump steak, thinly sliced
4 scallions, sliced diagonally

Soak the shiitake mushrooms in
1/2 cup boiling water for 10 minutes.
Place the noodles in a large,
heatproof bowl, cover with boiling
water, and allow them to rest for
5 minutes, then drain.

Heat the oil in a large saucepan, add
the leek, and cook over medium heat
for 3 minutes or until softened. Add
the chicken stock, dashi broth, soy
sauce, mirin, sugar, and mushrooms
and their soaking liquid. Bring to a
boil, then reduce the heat and
simmer for 5 minutes.

Add the cabbage and simmer for
another 5 minutes. Next, add the tofu
and beef and simmer for 5 minutes
or until the beef is cooked but still
tender. Divide the noodles among
the serving bowls and ladle on the
soup. Serve garnished with the
scallions.

Serves 4–6

# Pea and ham soup

1 lb. yellow or green split peas
1½ tablespoons olive oil
2 onions, chopped
1 carrot, diced
3 celery stalks, finely chopped
2 lbs. ham bones or a smoked hock, chopped
1 bay leaf
2 sprigs fresh thyme
lemon juice, to taste (optional)

Place the peas in a large bowl, cover with cold water, and soak for 6 hours. Drain well. Heat the oil in a large saucepan, add the onions, carrot, and celery, and cook over low heat for 6–7 minutes or until the vegetables are soft but not brown.

Add the split peas, ham bones, bay leaf, thyme, and 10 cups cold water and bring to a boil. Reduce the heat and simmer, stirring occasionally, for 2 hours or until the peas are tender. Discard the bay leaf and the sprigs of thyme.

Remove the ham bones from the soup and cool slightly. Remove the meat from the bone, discard the bones, and chop the meat. Return the ham to the soup and reheat. Season to taste with freshly ground pepper and lemon juice, if desired.

Serves 6–8

Note: For a finer texture, the soup can be cooled and processed before returning the meat to the saucepan. Variation: For a more hearty dish, heat sliced frankfurters or spicy smoked sausage in the cooked soup.

# Chicken and galangal soup

3/4 x 2-inch piece fresh galangal,
   peeled and cut into thin slices
2 cups coconut milk
1 cup chicken stock
4 fresh kaffir lime leaves, torn
1 tablespoon finely chopped fresh
   cilantro roots
1 lb. skinless, boneless chicken
   breasts, cut into thin strips
1–2 teaspoons finely chopped
   fresh red chilies
2 tablespoons fish sauce
1 1/2 tablespoons lime juice
3 teaspoons light brown sugar
4 tablespoons fresh cilantro leaves

Place the galangal in a saucepan with
the coconut milk, stock, lime leaves,
and cilantro roots. Bring to a boil,
reduce the heat to low, and simmer
for 10 minutes, stirring occasionally.

Add the chicken and chilies to the
saucepan and simmer for 8 minutes.

Stir in the fish sauce, lime juice, and
brown sugar and cook for 1 minute.
Stir in the cilantro leaves. Serve
immediately, garnished with extra
cilantro if desired.

Serves 4

## Lentil and Swiss chard soup

*Chicken stock*
2 lbs. chicken parts (necks, ribs, wings), fat removed
1 small onion, roughly chopped
1 bay leaf
3–4 sprigs fresh Italian parsley
1–2 sprigs fresh oregano or thyme

1½ cups brown lentils, washed
1¾ lbs. Swiss chard
¼ cup olive oil
1 large onion, finely chopped
4 cloves garlic, crushed
½ cup finely chopped fresh cilantro leaves
⅓ cup lemon juice
lemon wedges, to serve

To make the stock, place all the ingredients in a large saucepan, add 12 cups water, and bring to a boil. Skim any impurities from the surface. Reduce the heat and simmer for 2 hours. Strain the stock, discarding the chicken parts, onion, and herbs. (You will need 4 cups.) Chill overnight.

Skim any fat from the stock. Place the lentils in a large saucepan, then add the stock and 4 cups water. Bring to a boil, then reduce the heat and simmer, covered, for 1 hour.

Meanwhile, remove the stems from the Swiss chard and shred the leaves. Heat the oil in a saucepan over medium heat and cook the onion for 2–3 minutes or until transparent. Add the garlic and cook for 1 minute. Add the Swiss chard and toss for 2–3 minutes or until wilted. Stir the mixture into the lentils. Add the cilantro and lemon juice, season, and simmer, covered, for 15–20 minutes. Serve with the lemon wedges.

Serves 6

# Pork and glass noodle soup

5 oz. cellophane noodles
2 teaspoons peanut oil
2 teaspoons grated fresh ginger
5 cups chicken stock
1/3 cup Chinese rice wine
1 tablespoon hoisin sauce
1 tablespoon soy sauce
4 scallions, thinly sliced diagonally,
  plus extra to garnish
10 oz. sliced Chinese roast pork

Soak the noodles in a large bowl with enough boiling water to cover for 3–4 minutes. Drain.

Heat the oil in a large saucepan. Add the ginger and stir-fry for 1 minute. Add the stock, Chinese rice wine, hoisin and soy sauces, and simmer for 10 minutes. Add the scallions and roast pork, then cook for another 5 minutes.

Divide the noodles among 4 large bowls. Ladle in the soup and arrange the pork on top. Garnish with extra scallion slices.

Serves 4

# Cauliflower soup with smoked salmon croutons

*Croutons*
1 loaf day-old white bread, sliced
   lengthwise
2 tablespoons butter, melted
1 clove garlic, crushed
5 oz. smoked salmon
1 tablespoon finely chopped fresh dill

*Soup*
1 tablespoon oil
1 leek, white part only, chopped
1 clove garlic, chopped
3/4 lb. cauliflower, cut into florets
1 potato, chopped
1 cup chicken stock
1 cup milk
1 1/4 cups cream
1 tablespoon lemon juice
1 tablespoon horseradish cream
1 tablespoon chopped fresh chives

Preheat the oven to 300°F. Brush 3 slices of the bread on both sides with the combined butter and garlic, then season with salt. Cut off the crusts, cut each slice into 4 strips, then transfer the strips to a baking tray, spacing them a little apart. Bake for 30 minutes or until crisp and golden.

Meanwhile, heat the oil in a large saucepan, add the leek and garlic, and cook over medium heat for 6–8 minutes or until the leek is soft but not brown. Increase the heat to high, add the cauliflower, potato, stock, and milk, and bring just to a boil. Reduce the heat and simmer, covered, for 20 minutes or until the potato and cauliflower have softened.

Cool the mixture slightly, then transfer to a blender or food processor and purée until smooth. Return to a clean saucepan and add the cream, lemon, and horseradish. Reheat gently for 5 minutes, then add the chives.

Cut the salmon into strips the same width as the croutons and lay along the top of each crouton. Sprinkle with the dill. Serve the soup in deep bowls with two long croutons for each person.

Serves 4

## Curried chicken noodle soup

6 oz. dried, thin egg noodles
2 tablespoons peanut oil
2 chicken breasts, about 1/2 lb. each
1 onion, sliced
1 small fresh red chili, seeded and
  finely chopped
1 tablespoon finely chopped fresh
  ginger
2 tablespoons Indian curry powder
3 cups chicken stock
3 1/4 cups coconut milk
4 cups baby bok choy, cut into
  long strips
1/3 cup fresh basil, torn

Cook the noodles in a large saucepan of boiling water for 3–4 minutes or until cooked. Drain well and set aside. Wipe the saucepan clean and dry.

Heat the oil in the dry saucepan and add the chicken. Cook on each side for 5 minutes or until cooked through. Remove the chicken and keep warm.

Place the onion in the saucepan and cook over low heat for 8 minutes or until softened but not browned. Add the chili, ginger, and curry powder, and cook for another 2 minutes. Add the chicken stock and bring to a boil. Reduce the heat and simmer for 20 minutes. Thinly slice the chicken diagonally.

Add the coconut milk to the saucepan and simmer for 10 minutes. Add the bok choy and cook for 3 minutes, then stir in the basil.

To serve, divide the noodles among 4 deep serving bowls. Top with slices of chicken and ladle in the soup. Serve immediately.

Serves 4

# Seafood soup with rouille

*Rouille*
1 cooked russet potato, peeled
  and diced
1 red pepper, roasted and peeled
2 cloves garlic, chopped
1 egg yolk
1/2 cup olive oil

4 cups fish stock
1/2 teaspoon saffron threads
4 sprigs fresh thyme
2-inch piece orange rind
1 small French baguette
olive oil, for brushing
10 oz. salmon fillets, cut into 4 pieces
10 oz. firm white fish fillets, such as
  cod or halibut, cut into 4 pieces
1 squid body, cleaned and cut
  into rings
8 large shrimp, shelled and deveined

To make the rouille, place the potato, red pepper, garlic, and egg yolk in a food processor and process until smooth. With the motor running, gradually add the olive oil until the mixture has the consistency of mayonnaise.

Preheat the oven to 350°F. Place the stock in a large saucepan and bring to a boil. Add the saffron, thyme, and orange rind. Turn off the heat and allow to rest for 10 minutes while the flavors infuse.

Meanwhile, cut the baguette into 1/2-inch slices, brush with oil, and place on a baking tray. Bake for 10 minutes or until crisp and golden.

Strain the stock and return to a boil, then add the salmon and white fish fillets, squid rings, and shrimp. Remove the stock from the heat and leave for 2 minutes or until the seafood is cooked. Divide among 4 warm soup bowls and serve with the rouille and croutons.

Serves 4

## Ramen noodle soup with roast pork and greens

1/2 oz. dried shiitake mushrooms
3/4 lb. Chinese kale, trimmed and
   cut into 1 1/2-inch pieces
3/4 lb. fresh ramen noodles
6 cups chicken stock
3 tablespoons soy sauce
1 teaspoon sugar
3/4 lb. roast pork, thinly sliced
1 small, fresh red chili, seeded and
   thinly sliced

Soak the mushrooms in 1/2 cup hot water until softened. Squeeze the mushrooms dry, saving the liquid. Discard the hard stems and finely slice the caps.

Blanch the kale in a large saucepan of boiling salted water for 3 minutes or until tender but firm to the bite. Drain, then rinse in cold water.

Cook the noodles in a large saucepan of boiling water for 3 minutes or until just softened. Drain, rinse under cold water, then set aside.

Place the stock in a large saucepan and bring to a boil. Add the sliced mushrooms, mushroom liquid, soy sauce, and sugar. Simmer for 2 minutes, then add the kale.

Divide the noodles among 4 large bowls. Ladle on the hot stock and vegetables. Top with the pork and sliced chili. Serve hot.

Serves 4

# Salads

# Fresh tuna Niçoise

4 eggs
1¼ lbs. waxy potatoes, such as
   All Red or Butterfinger, peeled
1½ cups green beans
1½ lbs. tuna steaks, cut to
   ¾ inch thick
⅓ cup olive oil
2 tablespoons red wine vinegar
2 tablespoons chopped fresh
   Italian parsley
20 cherry tomatoes, halved
1 small red onion, thinly sliced
¾ cup pitted black olives

Place the eggs in a saucepan of cold water, bring to a boil, then reduce the heat and simmer for 4 minutes. Cool the eggs under cold running water, then peel and quarter.

Return the water to a boil, add the potatoes, then reduce the heat and simmer for 12 minutes or until tender. Remove. Add the beans to the saucepan and cook for 3–4 minutes or until tender but still bright green. Drain, rinse under cold water, and cut in half. Slice the potatoes thickly.

Rub pepper on both sides of the tuna. Sear on a barbecue or in a frying pan for 2 minutes on each side for rare, or until still pink in the middle. Cool slightly, then slice.

Combine the oil, vinegar, and parsley in a small pitcher. Gently toss the potatoes, beans, tomatoes, onion, and olives in a bowl, and season. Add three quarters of the dressing and toss well. Divide among 4 bowls, top with the tuna and egg, and drizzle with the remaining dressing.

Serves 4

## Orange sweet potato and fried noodle salad

2½ lbs. orange sweet potatoes,
  peeled and cut into ¾-inch chunks
2 tablespoons light oil
1⅓ cups roasted unsalted cashews
1 cup finely chopped fresh
  cilantro leaves
4-oz. packet fried noodles

*Dressing*
¾ teaspoon red curry paste
⅓ cup coconut milk
2 tablespoons lime juice
1½ tablespoons light brown sugar
2 tablespoons light oil
4 cloves garlic, finely chopped
1 tablespoon finely chopped fresh
  ginger

Preheat the oven to 400°F. Place the sweet potatoes and oil in a bowl and season lightly with salt and pepper. Toss together until well coated. Place on a baking sheet and bake for 30 minutes or until tender. Drain on crumpled paper towels.

To make the dressing, combine the curry paste, coconut milk, lime juice, and sugar in a food processor.

Heat the oil in a small frying pan. Add the garlic and ginger and cook over low heat for 1–2 minutes or until light brown. Remove and add to the dressing.

Place the sweet potatoes, cashews, cilantro, dressing, and the noodles in a large bowl and toss gently until combined. Serve immediately.

Serves 4–6

Note: This is best assembled just before serving, to keep the noodles from becoming soggy.

# Salmon and potato salad

1²/₃ lbs. salmon fillets
1³/₄ lbs. small red boiler potatoes,
  halved or quartered
3 tablespoons sour cream
1 tablespoon lemon juice
3 tablespoons mayonnaise
1 teaspoon Dijon mustard
1½ tablespoons horseradish
  cream
2 tablespoons finely chopped
  fresh dill
½ red onion, finely diced
vegetable oil, for brushing
8 romaine lettuce leaves
lemon wedges, to serve

Remove any bones from the salmon, then cut into ³/₄-inch slices. Chill. Boil the potatoes for 20 minutes or until tender. Drain and cool.

Combine the sour cream, lemon juice, mayonnaise, horseradish, and mustard. Place the potatoes, dill, and onion in a large bowl. Season, add the dressing, and toss to combine.

Heat a frying pan over high heat, brush with oil, and cook the salmon fillets for 1–2 minutes on each side. Remove from the pan.

Place 2 lettuce leaves in each of 4 serving bowls, spoon on the potatoes, and arrange the salmon slices over the top. Top with lemon wedges and ground black pepper.

Serves 4

# Fattoush

2 pita bread rounds (7-inch diameter)
6 romaine lettuce leaves, shredded
1 large cucumber, cubed
4 tomatoes, cut into ½-inch cubes
8 scallions, chopped
4 tablespoons finely chopped fresh
   Italian parsley
1 tablespoon finely chopped fresh
   mint
2 tablespoons finely chopped fresh
   cilantro

*Dressing*
2 cloves garlic, crushed
½ cup extra-virgin olive oil
½ cup lemon juice

Preheat the oven to 350°F. Split the bread in half through the center and bake on a cookie sheet for 8 minutes or until golden and crisp, turning halfway through. Break into pieces.

To make the dressing, whisk all the ingredients together in a bowl until well combined.

Place the bread and remaining salad ingredients in a serving bowl and toss to combine. Drizzle with the dressing and toss well. Season to taste with salt and freshly ground black pepper. Serve immediately.

Serves 6

Note: This is a popular Middle Eastern salad that is served as an appetizer or to accompany a light meal.

# Vietnamese chicken salad

3/4 lb. skinless, boneless chicken
  breasts
1 lemongrass stalk, white part only,
  finely chopped
1 tablespoon fish sauce
2 teaspoons sugar
2 tablespoons lime juice
1 1/2 tablespoons sweet chili sauce
4 1/2 cups Chinese cabbage
  (wom buk), thinly sliced
1 carrot, cut into ribbons with a
  vegetable peeler
1/2 small red onion, sliced
1/2 cup fresh cilantro leaves
1/2 cup roughly chopped fresh mint
2 tablespoons fresh cilantro leaves,
  extra
2 tablespoons chopped peanuts
1 tablespoon crisp, fried shallots

Place the chicken and lemongrass
in a deep frying pan of lightly salted
water. Bring to a boil, then reduce
the heat and simmer gently for
8–10 minutes or until the chicken
is just cooked through. Drain and
keep warm.

Place the fish sauce, sugar, lime
juice, and sweet chili sauce in a small
saucepan and stir over medium heat
for 1 minute or until the sugar has
dissolved. Remove from the heat.

Place the cabbage, carrot, onion,
cilantro, and mint in a large bowl and
toss together well. Drizzle over three
quarters of the warmed dressing,
toss to combine, and transfer to a
serving platter.

Slice the chicken thinly and
diagonally, arrange over the top
of the salad, and drizzle with the
remaining dressing. Garnish with
the extra cilantro leaves, chopped
peanuts, and fried shallots.
Serve immediately.

Serves 4

Variation: Instead of Chinese
cabbage, a large green papaya
may be used. Remove the skin
and finely shred the fruit.

# Squid salad

*Dressing*

2 large cloves garlic, crushed
2 teaspoons grated fresh ginger
3 small fresh red chilies, seeded
  and thinly sliced
2 tablespoons light brown sugar
2 tablespoons fish sauce
2 tablespoons lime juice
1/2 teaspoon sesame oil

1 lb. squid bodies, cleaned
6 fresh kaffir lime leaves
1 lemongrass stalk, white part only,
  chopped
3–4 red Asian shallots, thinly sliced
1 cucumber, cut in half lengthwise
  and thinly sliced
3 tablespoons chopped fresh
  cilantro leaves
1/3 cup fresh mint
1 small oak leaf or coral lettuce,
  leaves separated
fried red Asian shallot flakes,
  to garnish

To make the dressing, place the garlic, ginger, chilies, brown sugar, fish sauce, lime juice, sesame oil, and 1 tablespoon water in a small saucepan. Stir occasionally over low heat until the sugar has dissolved. Set aside.

Cut the squid in half lengthwise. Clean and remove any quills. Cut a crisscross pattern on the inside of the squid, taking care not to cut all the way through. Cut the squid into 1-inch pieces.

Place the kaffir lime leaves, lemongrass, and 5 cups water in a saucepan and bring to a boil. Reduce the heat and simmer for 5 minutes. Add half the squid pieces and cook for 30 seconds or until they begin to curl up and turn opaque. Remove with a slotted spoon and keep warm. Repeat with the remaining squid. Discard the lime leaves, lemongrass, and liquid.

Place the squid, shallots, cucumber, cilantro, mint, lettuce, and dressing in a large bowl and toss together. Serve garnished with the shallot flakes.

Serves 4

# Green papaya salad

3/4 lb. green papaya, peeled
  and seeded
3/4 cup snake beans, cut into
  3/4-inch pieces
2 cloves garlic
2 small fresh red chilies, chopped
5 teaspoons dried shrimp
8 cherry tomatoes, halved
1 1/2 cups fresh cilantro sprigs
1/4 cup chopped roasted peanuts

*Dressing*
3 tablespoons fish sauce
2 tablespoons tamarind purée
1 tablespoon lime juice
3 tablespoons light brown sugar

Grate the papaya, sprinkle with salt, and allow to rest for 30 minutes. Rinse well.

Cook the beans in boiling water for 3 minutes or until tender. Plunge into cold water, then drain.

To make the dressing, combine the fish sauce, tamarind purée, lime juice, and brown sugar in a small bowl.

Pound the garlic and chilies in a mortar and pestle until fine. Add the dried shrimp and pound until puréed. Add the papaya and snake beans and lightly pound for 1 minute. Add the tomatoes and pound briefly.

Combine the cilantro with the papaya mixture and spoon onto serving plates. Pour the dressing over the top. Sprinkle with the peanuts and, if desired, red chili slices.

Serves 6

# Fresh beet and goat cheese salad

2 lbs. fresh beets with leaves
1$^2$/$_3$ cups green beans
1 tablespoon red wine vinegar
2 tablespoons extra-virgin olive oil
1 clove garlic, crushed
1 tablespoon drained capers,
   coarsely chopped
3$^1$/$_2$ oz. goat cheese

Trim the leaves from the beets. Scrub the beets and wash the leaves well. Add the whole beets to a large saucepan of boiling water, reduce the heat and simmer, covered, for 30 minutes or until tender when pierced with the point of a knife. (The cooking time may vary depending on the size of the beets.)

Meanwhile, bring a saucepan of water to a boil, add the beans, and cook for 3 minutes or until just tender. Remove with a slotted spoon and plunge into a bowl of cold water. Drain well. Add the beet leaves to the same saucepan of boiling water and cook for 3–5 minutes or until the leaves and stalks are tender. Drain, plunge into a bowl of cold water, then drain again well. Drain and cool the beets, then peel and cut into thin wedges.

To make the dressing, put the red wine vinegar, oil, garlic, capers, $^1$/$_2$ teaspoon salt, and $^1$/$_2$ teaspoon pepper in a screw-top jar and shake.

To serve, divide the beans, beet leaves, and beets among 4 serving plates. Crumble goat cheese over the top and drizzle with the dressing.

Serves 4

# Crab and spinach soba noodle salad

¹/₄ cup Japanese rice vinegar
¹/₂ cup mirin
2 tablespoons soy sauce
1 teaspoon finely chopped fresh
ginger
8 cups spinach
¹/₂ lb. fresh cooked crabmeat
¹/₂ lb. soba noodles
2 teaspoons sesame oil
2 scallions, finely chopped
1 sheet nori, cut into matchstick-size
strips

Combine the rice vinegar, mirin, soy sauce, and ginger in a small bowl. Set aside.

Bring a large saucepan of salted water to a boil. Blanch the spinach for 15–20 seconds, then remove with a slotted spoon (set aside the water in the saucepan). Place the spinach in a bowl of ice-cold water for 30 seconds. Drain and squeeze out the moisture, then coarsely chop. Combine with the crabmeat and 2 tablespoons of the rice vinegar mixture.

Bring the saucepan of water back to a boil and cook the noodles for 5 minutes or until just tender. Drain, then rinse under cold water. Toss with the sesame oil, scallions, and the remaining dressing. Divide the noodles among individual bowls, top with the spinach and crabmeat, and sprinkle with nori.

Serves 4

# Shrimp and saffron potato salad

16 medium shrimp
1/3 cup olive oil
1 lb. new potatoes, cut in half
1/4 teaspoon saffron threads, crushed
1 clove garlic, crushed
1 bird's-eye chili, seeded and finely
  chopped
1 teaspoon grated lime zest
1/4 cup lime juice
6 cups baby arugula

Preheat the oven to 350°F. Peel and devein the shrimp, leaving the tails intact.

Heat 2 tablespoons of the oil in a frying pan and brown the potatoes. Transfer to a roasting pan and toss gently with the saffron and some salt and black pepper. Bake for 25 minutes or until tender.

Heat a ridged grill pan or skillet over medium heat. Toss the shrimp in a small bowl with the garlic, chili, lime zest, and 1 tablespoon of the oil. Cook the shrimp for 2 minutes each side or until pink and cooked.

In a small jar, shake up the lime juice and the remaining oil. Season with salt and pepper. Place the potatoes on a plate, top with the arugula and shrimp, and drizzle with dressing.

Serves 4

## Roasted fennel and orange salad

8 baby fennel bulbs
1/2 cup olive oil
1 teaspoon sea salt
2 oranges
1 tablespoon lemon juice
1 red onion, halved and thinly sliced
1/2 cup Kalamata olives
2 tablespoons chopped fresh mint
1 tablespoon roughly chopped fresh
   Italian parsley

Preheat the oven to 400°F. Trim and set aside the fennel leaves. Remove the stalks and cut a 1/4-inch slice off the bottom of each fennel. Cut each bulb into 6 wedges. Place in a flameproof dish and drizzle with 1/4 cup oil. Add the salt and plenty of pepper. Bake for 40–60 minutes or until the fennel is tender and slightly caramelized. Allow to cool.

Cut a slice off the top and bottom of each orange. Using a small, sharp knife, carefully remove the skin and as much pith as possible. Working over a bowl, cut down each side of a segment between the flesh and the membrane, and lift the segment out. Repeat with all the segments. Squeeze out any remaining juice from the membrane.

Whisk the remaining olive oil into the orange and lemon juice until emulsified. Season. Combine the orange segments, onion, and olives, pour on half the dressing, and mix in half the mint. Transfer to a serving dish and top with the roasted fennel. Drizzle with the remaining dressing and sprinkle with the parsley and the remaining mint. Roughly chop the feathery leaves and sprinkle over the salad.

Serves 4

# Pork, shrimp, and vermicelli salad in lettuce cups

vegetable oil, for frying
4 oz. dried rice vermicelli
3 tablespoons peanut oil
1 clove garlic, crushed
1 tablespoon finely chopped fresh ginger
3 scallions, finely sliced and green ends set aside for garnish
5 oz. ground pork
1 lb. shrimp, peeled, deveined, and roughly chopped
2 tablespoons Chinese rice wine
2 tablespoons soy sauce
2 tablespoons hoisin sauce
1 tablespoon brown bean sauce
1/2 teaspoon sugar
1/4 cup chicken stock
12 iceberg lettuce leaves, trimmed into cups

Fill a deep, heavy-bottomed saucepan one-third full of oil and heat to 325°F or until a cube of bread browns in 20 seconds. Add the vermicelli in batches and deep-fry until puffed up but not browned—this will only take a few seconds. Remove with a slotted spoon and drain on crumpled paper towels.

Heat the peanut oil in a wok over high heat and swirl to coat the side. Add the garlic, ginger, and scallions, and stir-fry for 1 minute, being careful not to burn the garlic.

Add the ground pork to the wok, breaking up the lumps, and cook for another 4 minutes. Add the shrimp and stir-fry for 2 minutes or until they begin to change color.

Add the Chinese rice wine, soy sauce, hoisin sauce, brown bean sauce, sugar, chicken stock, and 1/2 teaspoon salt and stir until combined. Cook over high heat for 2 minutes or until the mixture thickens slightly. Divide the noodles among the lettuce cups, top with the pork and shrimp mixture, and garnish with the scallion slices. Serve immediately.

Serves 6

# Chickpea and flatbread salad

3 pieces flatbread or tortilla
6 firm, ripe tomatoes, chopped
1½ red peppers, seeded and sliced
9 scallions, sliced
20 oz. canned chickpeas, rinsed
  and drained
½ cup olive oil
2 teaspoons grated lemon zest
¼ cup lemon juice
1½ teaspoons ground cumin
4 tablespoons chopped fresh
  Italian parsley

Preheat the oven to 400°F. Place the bread on a cookie sheet and bake for 8 minutes or until crisp. Cool, then break up into pieces.

Place the tomatoes, peppers, scallions, chickpeas, and bread pieces in a large bowl and toss gently. Combine the oil, lemon zest and juice, and cumin, and pour over the salad. Sprinkle the parsley over the top, mix well, and serve.

Serves 4

Note: This salad can be made in advance, but don't add the flatbread pieces until just prior to serving or they will become soggy.

# Roast duck and noodle salad

3/4 lb. fresh flat Chinese egg noodles
1 teaspoon sesame oil, plus
 1 tablespoon extra
1 tablespoon grated fresh ginger
1/2–1 teaspoon sambal oelek,
 or to taste
2 tablespoons fish sauce
2 tablespoons rice wine vinegar
1 tablespoon lime juice
1/4 teaspoon Chinese five-spice
 powder
1 tablespoon light brown sugar
2 tablespoons peanut oil
1 cup roughly chopped fresh cilantro,
 plus extra leaves to garnish
1 Chinese roast duck, meat removed
 from bones and sliced into bite-size
 pieces
2 cups bean sprouts
3 scallions, thinly sliced
1/2 cup roasted peanuts, chopped

Bring a large saucepan of lightly salted water to a boil. Add the noodles and cook for 3–4 minutes or until just tender. Rinse under cold water, drain, and toss with 1 teaspoon sesame oil.

Place the ginger, sambal oelek, fish sauce, vinegar, lime juice, five-spice powder, and sugar in a small bowl and stir to dissolve the sugar. Whisk in the extra sesame oil and the peanut oil, then stir in the cilantro. Season to taste with salt.

Place the noodles, duck, bean sprouts, and scallions in a large bowl. Pour on the dressing and toss to coat. Season to taste. Garnish with the chopped peanuts and extra cilantro leaves.

Serves 4

# Smoked trout Caesar salad

3/4 lb. smoked trout fillets, skin
  removed
2 1/2 cups green beans, halved
6 canned artichokes, drained, rinsed,
  and quartered
2 eggs
1 small clove garlic, chopped
2 teaspoons Dijon mustard
2 tablespoons white wine vinegar
1/3 cup olive oil
6 slices day-old, Italian-style bread,
  cut into 3/4-inch cubes
2 tablespoons capers, drained
1 head romaine lettuce, leaves
  separated
1/2 cup freshly shaved Parmesan

Flake the trout into 1 1/2-inch shards
and place in a bowl. Cook the beans
in boiling water for 3 minutes or until
tender and still bright green. Rinse
under cold water. Add to the bowl
with the artichokes.

Poach the eggs in simmering water
for 40 seconds or until just cooked.
Place in a food processor with the
garlic, mustard, and vinegar, and
process until smooth. With the
motor running, add 2 tablespoons
oil in a thin stream, processing until
thick and creamy. Season to taste.

Heat the remaining oil in a frying
pan, add the bread and capers, and
cook over high heat for 3–5 minutes
or until golden. Line 4 bowls with the
romaine leaves. Divide the trout
mixture among the bowls, drizzle with
the dressing, and top with the
croutons, capers, and Parmesan.

Serves 4

# Shrimp salad with Asian dressing

*Dressing*
1/3 cup rice vinegar
1/4 cup soy sauce
2 tablespoons honey
1 teaspoon sesame oil
1–2 teaspoons grated fresh ginger
2 cloves garlic, crushed

2 carrots (1²/³ cups), cut into thin
  2-inch-long strips
1 red pepper, thinly sliced
1/2 cup daikon radish, peeled and
  cut into thin 2-inch-long strips
small bunch chives, cut into 2-inch
  pieces
1 1/2 lbs. cooked medium shrimp,
  peeled and deveined, with tails
  intact
4 cups baby spinach leaves

Place all the dressing ingredients in a small saucepan and warm over medium heat for 2–3 minutes or until the honey dissolves; do not boil. Remove the saucepan from the heat.

Place the thin strips of carrot, the pepper, radish, and chives in a bowl and toss with tongs to distribute evenly. Add the shrimp to the vegetables, pour on half the dressing, then toss thoroughly again.

To assemble the salad, make a bed of spinach on four plates (or a platter), place the mixed vegetable strips and shrimp on the spinach, and drizzle with the remaining dressing. Serve immediately.

Serves 4

## Pork and udon noodle salad with lime dressing

*Dressing*
⅓ cup lime juice
1 tablespoon sesame oil
2 tablespoons ponzu (Japanese
  dipping sauce)
¼ cup honey

¾ lb. fresh udon noodles
1 lb. pork fillet
1 tablespoon sesame oil
1¼ cups roasted unsalted peanuts
2 large fresh red chilies, seeded
  and finely diced
2 teaspoons finely chopped fresh
  ginger
1 large cucumber, peeled, halved,
  seeds removed, and julienned
2¼ cups bean sprouts
½ cup chopped fresh cilantro leaves

Preheat the oven to 400°F. To make the dressing, place the lime juice, sesame oil, ponzu, and honey in a screw-top jar and shake.

Cook the noodles in a saucepan of boiling water for 1–2 minutes or until tender. Drain, rinse, and set aside.

Trim the fat and sinew off the pork and brush with the sesame oil. Season. Heat a nonstick frying pan until very hot and cook the pork for 5–6 minutes or until browned on all sides. Remove from the pan and allow to rest for 5 minutes.

Combine the noodles, peanuts, chilies, ginger, cucumber, bean sprouts, and cilantro, and toss well. Cut the pork into thin slices, add to the salad with the dressing, and toss before serving.

Serves 4

# Tuna, tomato, and arugula pasta salad

¾ lb. dried fettucine
¾ lb. tuna steaks
½ cup sun-dried tomatoes, drained
  and roughly chopped, saving
  2 tablespoons oil
2 cloves garlic, crushed
½ cup sun-dried peppers, drained
  and roughly chopped
⅔ cup capers, drained
1 cup black olives, pitted and
  quartered
3 cups baby arugula leaves

Bring a large saucepan of lightly salted water to a boil. Add the pasta and cook until al dente. Drain. Meanwhile, lightly brush a ridged grill pan or skillet with oil and cook the tuna for 1–2 minutes each side (it should be rare in the center). Cut the tuna into 1-inch cubes. Keep warm.

Heat the sun-dried tomato oil in a saucepan over medium heat. Add the tomatoes, garlic, peppers, capers, and olives, and cook, stirring, for 5–6 minutes or until the mixture is heated through.

Place the pasta, tomato mixture, and arugula in a large bowl, season, and toss to combine. Divide among 4 serving plates and top with the tuna. Serve with lemon wedges and shaved Parmesan, if desired.

Serves 4

Note: If you prefer the tuna rare, use very fresh sashimi tuna. If baby arugula leaves are not available, use larger arugula leaves and tear them into pieces.

# Lamb and rice noodle salad with peanut dressing

1 lb. lamb fillet, cut lengthwise
   into thin strips
2 tablespoons light soy sauce
1 tablespoon rice wine
1/4 lb. dried rice noodle sticks
1 cucumber, unpeeled, cut into long
   thin strips with a vegetable peeler
2/3 cup unsalted toasted peanuts,
   chopped
fresh cilantro sprigs, to garnish

*Spicy peanut dressing*
3 cloves garlic
3/4 cup smooth peanut butter
4 tablespoons soy sauce
1 cup fresh cilantro leaves
1 tablespoon rice wine vinegar
1 tablespoon Chinese rice wine
   or dry sherry
2 tablespoons light brown sugar
1 small fresh red chili, roughly
   chopped

Combine the lamb, soy sauce, and rice wine in a bowl. Cover and marinate for 1 hour.

To make the peanut dressing, purée all the ingredients with 2 tablespoons water in a blender until smooth.

Soak the noodles in a bowl of boiling water for 15 minutes. Drain, then rinse under cold water.

Heat a grill until very hot and sear the lamb slices in batches for 30 seconds on each side, then transfer to a large bowl. Add the noodles, cucumber, and three quarters of the dressing, and toss to combine. Serve on a dish and drizzle with the remaining dressing. Sprinkle with the peanuts and garnish with the cilantro sprigs.

Serves 4

# Grilled baby octopus salad

2-lb. baby octopus
1 teaspoon sesame oil
2 tablespoons lime juice
2 tablespoons fish sauce
1/4 cup sweet chili sauce
6 handfuls mixed salad leaves
1 red pepper, very thinly sliced
2 small cucumbers, seeded and
  cut into ribbons
4 red Asian shallots, chopped
2/3 cup roasted, unsalted peanuts,
  chopped

To clean the octopus, remove the head from the tentacles by cutting just underneath the eyes. To clean the head, carefully slit the head open and remove the gut. Cut it in half. Push out the beak from the center of the tentacles, then cut the tentacles into sets of four or two, depending on their size. Pull the skin away from the head and tentacles if it comes away easily. The eyes will come off as you pull off the skin.

To make the marinade, combine the sesame oil, lime juice, fish sauce, and chili sauce in a shallow, nonmetallic bowl. Add the octopus and stir to coat. Cover and chill for 2 hours.

Heat a ridged grill pan, skillet, or barbecue until very hot. Drain the octopus, setting aside the marinade, then cook in batches for 3 minutes or until cooked, turning occasionally.

Pour the marinade into a small saucepan, bring to a boil, and cook for 2 minutes or until it has slightly thickened.

Divide the salad leaves among plates, sprinkle with slices of pepper and cucumber, then top with the octopus. Drizzle with the marinade and top with the Asian shallots and peanuts.

Serves 4 as an appetizer

# Shrimp, prosciutto, and arugula salad

4 Roma tomatoes, quartered
  lengthwise
1 clove garlic, chopped
1/3 cup olive oil
8 slices prosciutto
20 medium shrimp, peeled, deveined,
  and cut in half lengthwise
2 teaspoons balsamic vinegar
2 avocados, pits removed, thinly
  sliced
1 1/2 cups baby arugula leaves

Preheat the oven to 275°F. Place the tomato quarters in a bowl and toss with the garlic, 1 tablespoon of the oil, and some salt and pepper. Place the tomato quarters on a baking tray and roast for 1 1/2 hours. Remove from the oven.

Lightly brush the prosciutto with a little of the remaining olive oil. Heat a nonstick frying pan over medium–high heat. When hot, add the prosciutto in two batches, cooking for 3–4 minutes each side until it starts to become crisp. Drain on paper towels to remove any excess oil, then break into pieces.

Heat a ridged grill pan or skillet until it is hot, lightly oil the pan, then cook the shrimp in batches for 2 minutes on each side. Season well and transfer to a large serving bowl.

Combine the rest of the olive oil with the balsamic vinegar. To assemble the salad, place the tomatoes, prosciutto, avocado, and arugula in the bowl with the shrimp. Drizzle with 1 tablespoon of the dressing, then gently toss together. Drizzle with the remaining dressing and serve.

Serves 4

# Thai beef salad

1 lb. rump steak
3½ tablespoons lime juice
2 tablespoons fish sauce
1 teaspoon light brown sugar
2 cloves garlic, crushed
1 lcmongrass stalk, white part
  only, finely sliced
2 small fresh red chilies, finely sliced
4 red Asian shallots, finely sliced
15–20 fresh mint leaves
½ cup fresh cilantro leaves
¼ lb. cherry tomatoes, halved
1 cucumber, halved lengthwise and
  thinly sliced
3 cups shredded Chinese cabbage
¼ cup store-bought Asian fried
  onions
1 tablespoon store-bought Asian
  fried garlic
¼ cup crushed peanuts, to garnish

Heat a nonstick frying pan over medium-high heat until very hot. Cook the steak for 4 minutes each side, then remove and cool.

Combine the lime juice, fish sauce, brown sugar, garlic, lemongrass, and chili, and stir to dissolve the sugar. Add the shallots, mint, and cilantro. Thinly slice the beef across the grain and toss through the mixture. Chill for 15 minutes. Add the tomatoes and cucumber and toss well. Arrange the cabbage on a serving platter and top with the beef mixture. Sprinkle with the fried onions, garlic, and crushed peanuts.

Serves 4

# Greek salad

4 tomatoes, cut into wedges
1 cucumber, peeled, halved, seeded, and cut into small cubes
2 green peppers, seeded, halved lengthwise, and cut into strips
1 red onion, finely sliced
16 Kalamata olives
1/2 lb. good-quality, firm feta cheese, cut into cubes
3 tablespoons fresh Italian parsley
12 fresh mint leaves
1/2 cup extra-virgin olive oil
2 tablespoons lemon juice
1 clove garlic, crushed

Place the tomatoes, cucumber, peppers, onion, olives, feta, and half the parsley and mint leaves in a large salad bowl, and gently mix together.

Place the oil, juice, and garlic in a screw-top jar, season, and shake until combined. Pour the dressing over the salad and toss lightly. Garnish with the remaining parsley and mint.

Serves 4

# Asian salmon and noodle salad

½ cup lime juice
2 tablespoons grated fresh ginger
1 lb. fresh salmon fillet, skin and
  bones removed, thinly sliced
1¼ lbs. fresh egg noodles
2 tablespoons mirin
2 tablespoons fish sauce
2 teaspoons light brown sugar
¼ cup peanut oil
2 teaspoons sesame oil
1 small fresh red chili, chopped
8 scallions, sliced
2 tablespoons whole fresh cilantro
  leaves
1 tablespoon fresh Vietnamese mint,
  finely chopped
2 tablespoons chopped fresh garlic
  chives
fresh cilantro leaves, to garnish

Combine the lime juice and ginger
in a bowl, add the salmon, and toss
to coat. Refrigerate for a maximum
of 2 hours.

Cook the noodles in boiling water
for 2–3 minutes. Drain and rinse
in cold water.

Remove the fish from the marinade.
Add the mirin, fish sauce, brown
sugar, peanut and sesame oils, and
chili to the marinade. Mix well. Place
the noodles, fish, scallions, and
fresh herbs in a large bowl, add the
dressing, and toss to coat. Garnish
with the cilantro leaves.

Serves 4

# Pear and walnut salad with lime vinaigrette

1 small French baguette, cut into
   16 thin slices
oil, for brushing
1 clove garlic, cut in half
1 cup walnuts
1 1/2 cups cheese
8 cups mixed lettuce leaves
2 pears, cut into 3/4-inch cubes,
   mixed with 2 tablespoons lime juice

*Lime vinaigrette*
3 tablespoons extra virgin olive oil
1/4 cup lime juice
2 tablespoons raspberry vinegar

Preheat the oven to 350°F. Brush the baguette slices with a little oil, rub with the cut side of the garlic, then place on a baking tray. Bake for 10 minutes or until crisp and golden. Place the walnuts on a baking tray and roast for 5 minutes or until just slightly browned—shake the tray to ensure even browning. Allow to cool for 5 minutes.

To make the lime vinaigrette, whisk together the oil, lime juice, raspberry vinegar, 1 teaspoon salt, and 1/2 teaspoon ground black pepper in a bowl. Set aside until ready to use.

Spread some of the cheese on each crouton, then cook under a hot broiler for 2–3 minutes or until hot.

Place the lettuce, pears, and walnuts in a bowl, add the vinaigrette, and toss through. Divide the salad among 4 serving bowls and serve with the cheese croutons.

Serves 4

## Vietnamese shrimp and cabbage salad

1/3 cup rice vinegar
2 tablespoons fish sauce
2 tablespoons lime juice
2 tablespoons light brown sugar
1 small fresh red chili, seeded
 and finely chopped
2 tablespoons peanut oil
1 clove garlic, crushed
20 medium shrimp, peeled and
 deveined, with tails intact
2 cups thinly sliced cabbage
2 cups thinly sliced red cabbage
3/4 cup sliced drained bamboo shoots
1/2 cup fresh mint leaves
1/2 cup fresh cilantro leaves
2 fresh long green chilies, seeded and
 sliced thinly and diagonally
lime wedges, to serve

To make the salad dressing, combine the rice vinegar, fish sauce, lime juice, brown sugar, and red chili in a small bowl and stir together until the sugar has dissolved.

Heat the peanut oil in a nonstick frying pan or wok over medium heat. When hot, add the garlic and cook for 10 seconds, stirring constantly. Add the shrimp in two batches and cook for about 2 minutes on each side or until pink and cooked through, then remove from the pan.

Place the cabbage, bamboo shoots, herbs, and green chilies in a serving bowl and mix together well. Add the shrimp to the bowl, drizzle the dressing over the salad, season with pepper, and toss well. Serve with lime wedges.

Serves 4

## Chicken Waldorf salad

3 cups chicken stock
2 skinless, boneless chicken breasts
2 red apples
2 green apples
2 celery stalks, sliced
1 cup toasted walnuts
1/2 cup mayonnaise
1/4 cup sour cream
1/2 teaspoon chopped fresh tarragon
1 head romaine lettuce

Bring the stock to a boil in a medium saucepan. Remove from the heat, add the chicken to the stock, then cover and allow to cool in the liquid for 10 minutes, by which time the chicken should be cooked. Test by touching with your finger—the chicken should feel quite springy.

Cut the apples into bite-size pieces. Shred the chicken breasts and place in a large bowl with the apple, celery, walnuts, mayonnaise, sour cream, and tarragon. Season with salt and freshly ground black pepper and toss well to combine. Separate the lettuce leaves and arrange them in a serving bowl. Pile the Waldorf salad over the lettuce and serve.

Serves 4

# Pasta

## Creamy chicken and peppercorn pappardelle

2 skinless, boneless chicken breasts
  (14 oz. total)
2 tablespoons butter
1 onion, halved and thinly sliced
2 tablespoons drained green
  peppercorns, slightly crushed
1/2 cup white wine
1 1/4 cups cream
3/4 lb. fresh pappardelle pasta
1/3 cup sour cream (optional)
2 tablespoons chopped fresh chives

Cut the chicken in half so that you have 4 flat fillets, and season with salt and pepper. Melt the butter in a frying pan, add the chicken, and cook for 3 minutes on each side or until lightly browned and cooked through. Remove from the pan, cut into slices, and keep warm.

Add the onion and peppercorns to the same pan and cook over medium heat for 3 minutes or until the onion has softened slightly. Add the wine and cook for 1 minute or until reduced by half. Stir in the cream and cook for 4–5 minutes or until thickened slightly, then season with salt and black pepper. Meanwhile, cook the pasta in a large saucepan of boiling water until al dente, then drain. Mix together the pasta, chicken, any juices, and the cream sauce. Divide the pasta among serving bowls, top with a dollop of sour cream, and sprinkle with chives.

Serves 4

## Angel-hair pasta with garlic, scallops, and arugula

20 sea scallops with roe
1/2 lb. angel-hair pasta
1/2 cup extra-virgin olive oil
2 cloves garlic, finely chopped
1/4 cup white wine
1 tablespoon lemon juice
3 cups baby arugula leaves
1/2 cup chopped fresh cilantro leaves

Trim any veins, membrane, or hard white muscle from the scallops. Pat dry with paper towels. Bring a large saucepan of water to a boil, add the pasta, and cook until al dente. Drain the pasta well and toss with 1 tablespoon oil.

Meanwhile, heat 1 tablespoon oil in a frying pan, add the garlic, and cook for a few seconds or until fragrant. Do not brown. Add the combined wine and lemon juice and remove from the heat.

Heat a ridged grill pan or skillet over high heat and brush with a little oil. Season the scallops with salt and pepper and cook for 1 minute on each side or until just cooked. Gently reheat the garlic mixture, add the arugula, and stir over medium heat for 1–2 minutes or until wilted. Toss through the pasta, then add the remaining oil and half the cilantro and mix well. Divide the pasta among 4 serving bowls, arrange the scallops over the top, and garnish with the remaining cilantro.

Serves 4

Variation: Add 1/2 teaspoon dried chili flakes just before the wine and lemon juice for an extra kick.

## Macaroni & cheese with pancetta

2½ cups macaroni
2½ oz. pancetta, diced
2 cups cream
1 cup grated cheddar
2 cups grated Gruyère
1 cup grated Parmesan
1 clove garlic, crushed
2 teaspoons Dijon mustard
½ teaspoon paprika
2 tablespoons chopped fresh chives
fresh chives, extra, to garnish

Bring a large saucepan of lightly salted water to a boil. Add the macaroni and cook until al dente. Drain, cover, and keep warm.

Meanwhile, place the pancetta in a large saucepan and cook over high heat, stirring, for 4 minutes or until well-browned and slightly crisp. Drain on paper towels. Reduce the heat to medium, stir in the cream, and simmer. Add the cheeses, garlic, mustard, and paprika, and stir for 5 minutes or until the cheeses have melted and the sauce has thickened. Season.

Add the macaroni and pancetta and stir for 1 minute or until heated through. Stir in the chives, garnish with the extra chives, and serve.

Serves 4

# Pasta with seared shrimp

8 large shrimp
2 tablespoons olive oil
1/3 cup unsalted butter, chopped
1 1/2 tablespoons drained baby capers
1/2 lb. angel-hair pasta
1/4 cup lemon juice
1 teaspoon grated lemon zest
1–2 small fresh red chilies, seeded
  and thinly sliced
1/2 cup chopped fresh Italian parsley
lemon wedges, to serve

Remove the heads from the shrimp. Slice them down the back without cutting right through, then open them out, leaving the tails and shells intact. Rinse under cold water and pull out the vein. Pat dry, then season lightly.

Heat the oil and half the butter in a large frying pan, add the capers, and cook for 1 minute. Remove from the pan and set aside. Add the shrimp and cook, cut-side down first, for 2–3 minutes each side or until pink. Remove and keep warm.

Cook the pasta in a saucepan of boiling water until al dente. Drain, setting aside 1–2 tablespoons of the cooking liquid.

Melt the remaining butter in the frying pan, add the lemon juice and zest, capers, and chilies, and stir until fragrant. Add the pasta and parsley and toss until the pasta is coated with the butter. If needed, add some of the cooking liquid to moisten the pasta. Season.

Divide the pasta among serving bowls, top with the shrimp, and serve with lemon wedges.

Serves 2 as a main course or
4 as an appetizer

# Peppered pork, zucchini, and garganelli

1 lb. pork fillet
3–4 teaspoons cracked black
  peppercorns
1/3 cup butter
1/2 lb. garganelli, penne, or
  fusilli pasta
1 onion, halved and thinly sliced
2 large zucchini, thinly sliced
2/3 cup fresh basil, torn
3/4 cup baby black olives
1/2 cup grated Romano cheese

Cut the pork fillet in half widthwise and roll in the pepper and some salt. Heat half the butter in a large frying pan, add the pork, and cook for 4 minutes on each side or until golden brown and just cooked through. Remove from the pan and cut into 1/4-inch slices, then set aside and keep warm.

Cook the pasta in a large saucepan of boiling water until al dente; drain well and return to the saucepan.

Meanwhile, melt the remaining butter in the frying pan, add the onion, and cook, stirring, over medium heat for about 3 minutes or until soft. Add the zucchini and toss for 5 minutes or until starting to soften. Add the basil, olives, and the sliced pork and any juices, and toss well. Stir the pork mixture through the hot pasta, then season to taste with salt and cracked black pepper. Serve immediately, topped with the cheese.

Serves 4

# Spaghetti with olive, caper, and anchovy sauce

¾ lb. spaghetti
⅓ cup olive oil
2 onions, finely chopped
3 cloves garlic, finely chopped
½ teaspoon chili flakes
6 large ripe tomatoes, diced
4 tablespoons capers in brine,
  rinsed and drained
7–8 anchovies in oil, drained
  and minced
1 cup Kalamata olives
3 tablespoons chopped fresh
  Italian parsley

Bring a large saucepan of salted water to a boil, add the spaghetti, and cook until al dente. Drain.

Meanwhile, heat the oil in a large saucepan, add the onions, and cook over medium heat for 5 minutes. Add the garlic and chili flakes and cook for 30 seconds, then add the tomatoes, capers, and anchovies. Simmer over low heat for 8 minutes or until thick and pulpy, then stir in the olives and parsley.

Stir the pasta through the sauce. Season with salt and freshly ground black pepper and serve immediately with crusty bread.

Serves 6

# Creamy pasta gnocchi with peas and prosciutto

3½ oz. thinly sliced prosciutto
3 teaspoons olive oil
2 eggs
1 cup cream
⅓ cup finely grated Parmesan
2 tablespoons chopped fresh
    Italian parsley
1 tablespoon chopped fresh chives
½ lb. fresh or frozen peas
1 lb. pasta gnocchi

Cut the prosciutto into ¼-inch-wide strips. Heat the oil in a frying pan over medium heat, add the prosciutto, and cook for 2 minutes or until crisp. Drain on paper towels. Place the eggs, cream, Parmesan, and herbs in a bowl and whisk well.

Bring a saucepan of salted water to a boil. Add the peas and cook for 5 minutes or until just tender. Leaving the saucepan on the heat, use a slotted spoon to transfer the peas to the bowl of cream mixture, then add ¼ cup of the cooking liquid to the same bowl. Using a potato masher or the back of a fork, roughly mash the peas.

Add the gnocchi to the boiling water and cook until al dente. Drain well, then return to the saucepan. Add the cream mixture and warm through over low heat, gently stirring for about 30 seconds until the gnocchi is coated in the sauce. Season to taste with salt and pepper. Divide among warmed plates, top with the prosciutto, and serve immediately.

Serves 4

Note: Be careful not to overheat the sauce, as the egg will begin to set and the result will look like a scrambled-egg sauce.

## Roast squash, feta, and arugula penne

2½ lbs. butternut squash, peeled and
  cut into ¾-inch cubes
1 teaspoon fresh rosemary
4 cloves garlic, crushed
2 tablespoons olive oil
1 lb. penne
1 tablespoon butter
1 large red onion, sliced
1 tablespoon honey
½ cup chicken stock
1⅓ cups feta, crumbled
3 cups fresh arugula leaves
shaved Parmesan, to garnish

Preheat the oven to 400°F. Place
the squash in a roasting pan with the
rosemary, garlic, and 1 tablespoon
olive oil, and toss to coat. Bake for
30 minutes or until the squash is soft
and golden. Season.

Meanwhile, cook the penne in
a large saucepan of lightly salted
boiling water until al dente. Drain,
return to the saucepan, and stir in
the butter. Keep warm.

Heat the remaining oil in a frying pan
over medium heat, add the onion,
and cook for 3–5 minutes, then add
the honey and cook for 2 minutes
or until the onion starts to caramelize.
Add the stock and simmer gently for
5–7 minutes or until reduced slightly.

Add the roast squash to the onion
mixture, stir to combine, then add
to the pasta with the feta and
arugula. Toss to combine and season
to taste. Garnish with the Parmesan.

Serves 4

## Cavatelli with pecorino and an herb sauce

3/4 lb. cavatelli pasta
1/3 cup butter
2 cloves garlic, crushed
3 tablespoons chopped fresh chives
3 tablespoons shredded fresh basil
1 tablespoon shredded fresh sage
1 teaspoon fresh thyme
1/4 cup warm vegetable stock
2/3 cup firmly packed grated pecorino
  cheese (see Note)

Cook the pasta in a large saucepan of rapidly boiling water until al dente. Meanwhile, heat the butter in a small saucepan over medium heat, add the garlic, and cook for 1 minute or until fragrant. Add the chives, basil, sage, and thyme, and cook for another minute.

Drain the pasta and return to the saucepan. Add the herb mixture and stock. Return to the heat for 2–3 minutes or until warmed through. Season to taste with salt and cracked black pepper. Add the grated pecorino and stir until well combined. Divide among 4 warm serving bowls and garnish with sage leaves if desired.

Serves 4

Note: Pecorino is made from sheep's milk and has a sharp flavor. If it is unavailable, use Parmesan.

# Tortellini boscaiola

2 tablespoons butter
4 bacon slices, chopped
2 cloves garlic, crushed
1 small leek, thinly sliced
3 cups portobello or button
  mushrooms, sliced
1/4 cup dry white wine
1 1/2 cups whipping cream
1 teaspoon chopped fresh thyme
1 lb. fresh veal tortellini
1/2 cup grated Parmesan
1 tablespoon chopped fresh
  Italian parsley

Melt the butter in a large frying pan, add the bacon, and cook over medium heat for 5 minutes or until crisp. Add the garlic and leek and cook for 2 minutes, then add the mushrooms and cook for 8 minutes or until softened. Add the wine, cream, and thyme, bring to a boil, then reduce the heat and simmer for 10 minutes or until the sauce has thickened.

Meanwhile, cook the tortellini in a large saucepan of lightly salted boiling water until al dente. Drain. Add the Parmesan to the sauce and stir over low heat until melted. Season. Combine the sauce with the tortellini and parsley.

Serves 4–6

## Cajun scallops, conchigliette, and buttery corn sauce

3/4 lb. conchigliette
  (small pasta shells)
20 large scallops, without roe
2 tablespoons Cajun spice mix
2 tablespoons corn oil
1 cup butter
3 cloves garlic, crushed
12-oz. can corn, drained
1/4 cup lime juice
4 tablespoons finely chopped fresh
  cilantro leaves

Cook the pasta in a large saucepan of boiling water until al dente. Drain and return to the saucepan to keep warm. Meanwhile, pat the scallops dry with paper towels and lightly coat in the spice mix. Heat the oil in a large frying pan and cook the scallops for 1 minute on each side over high heat (ensuring they are well spaced), then remove from the saucepan, cover, and keep warm.

Reduce the heat to medium, add the butter, and cook for 4 minutes or until foaming and golden brown. Remove from the heat and add the garlic, corn, and lime juice. Gently toss the corn mixture through the pasta with 2 tablespoons of the cilantro and season well. Divide among 4 serving plates, top with the scallops, drizzle with any juices, and sprinkle with the remaining cilantro.

Serves 4

Notes: Scallops should not be crowded in the pan or they will stew and become tough.
To achieve the most delicious flavors, don't use a nonstick frying pan—it will keep the butter from browning properly and the juices from caramelizing.

## Rotelle with chickpeas, tomatoes, and parsley

¾ lb. rotelle pasta
1 tablespoon ground cumin
½ cup olive oil
1 red onion, halved and thinly sliced
3 cloves garlic, crushed
13-oz. can chickpeas, drained
3 large tomatoes, diced
½ cup chopped fresh Italian parsley
¼ cup lemon juice

Cook the pasta in a large saucepan of boiling water until al dente. Drain and return to the saucepan.

Meanwhile, heat a large frying pan over medium heat, add the cumin, and cook, tossing, for 1 minute or until fragrant. Remove from the saucepan. Heat half the oil in the same saucepan and cook the onion over medium heat for 2–3 minutes or until soft. Stir in the garlic, chickpeas, tomatoes, and parsley, and stir until warmed through. Gently toss through the pasta.

Place the lemon juice, cumin, and remaining oil in a screw-top jar and shake together well. Add the dressing to the saucepan with the pasta and chickpea mixture, return to the stovetop over low heat, and stir until warmed through. Season well with salt and cracked black pepper. Serve hot or cold with grated Parmesan. If serving cold, rinse the pasta before adding the chickpea mixture and do not return to the heat.

Serves 4

# Spaghetti marinara

1 tablespoon olive oil
1 onion, chopped
3 cloves garlic, crushed
2 13-oz. cans crushed tomatoes
2 tablespoons tomato paste
$^2/_3$ cup dry white wine
2 teaspoons light brown sugar
1 teaspoon finely grated lemon zest
2 tablespoons chopped fresh basil
12 medium shrimp, peeled and
   deveined
12 large white scallops, without roe
2 small squid bodies (10 oz. total),
   cleaned and cut into $^1/_2$-inch rings
10 oz. spaghetti
2 tablespoons finely chopped fresh
   Italian parsley
shaved Parmesan, to serve

Heat the oil in a large saucepan, add the onion, and cook over medium heat for 5–8 minutes or until golden. Add the garlic, tomatoes, tomato paste, wine, sugar, lemon zest, half the basil, and 1 cup water. Cook for 1 hour, stirring occasionally, or until the sauce is reduced and thickened. Season with salt and pepper.

Add the shrimp and cook for 1 minute, then add the scallops and cook for 2 minutes. Stir in the calamari and cook for another minute or until all of the seafood is cooked through and tender.

Meanwhile, cook the spaghetti in lightly salted boiling water until al dente. Drain, then toss with the sauce, parsley, and remaining basil. Serve topped with shaved Parmesan.

Serves 4

# Shrimp, ricotta, and spinach pasta

3 firm, ripe tomatoes, peeled, seeded, and finely chopped
1/2 cup extra-virgin olive oil
1/2 cup balsamic vinegar
3 cloves garlic, finely chopped
3 tablespoons finely chopped fresh basil
1 lb. penne rigate
1 tablespoon olive oil
1 3/4 lbs. raw medium shrimp, peeled and deveined, with tails intact
2 cups baby spinach leaves
3/4 cup firm ricotta, crumbled
2 tablespoons shaved Parmesan

Combine the tomatoes, extra-virgin olive oil, 2 tablespoons of the balsamic vinegar, 1 clove of the garlic, and 2 tablespoons of the basil.

Cook the pasta in a large saucepan of boiling water until al dente. Drain and keep warm.

Meanwhile, heat the olive oil in a frying pan over high heat, stir in the remaining garlic, then add the shrimp and cook over high heat for 1–2 minutes or until the shrimp turn pink. Add the remaining vinegar and basil and cook for 1–2 minutes or until the liquid has reduced and the shrimp are cooked and slightly glazed. Stir in the spinach until just wilted. Season.

Toss together everything except the cheeses. Divide among bowls and top with the ricotta and Parmesan.

Serves 4

# Penne with rustic lentil sauce

4 cups chicken stock
3/4 lb. penne
1/3 cup extra-virgin olive oil,
  plus extra for drizzling
1 onion, chopped
2 carrots, diced
3 celery stalks, diced
3 cloves garlic, crushed
1 tablespoon plus 1 teaspoon
  chopped fresh thyme
13-oz. can lentils, drained, or
  2 1/2 cups cooked brown lentils

Boil the chicken stock in a large saucepan for 10 minutes or until reduced to 2 cups of liquid. Cook the pasta in a large saucepan of rapidly boiling water for 10 minutes or until al dente. Drain and toss with 2 tablespoons of the olive oil.

Heat the remaining oil in a large, deep frying pan, add the onion, carrots, and celery, and cook over medium heat for 10 minutes or until browned. Add two thirds of the crushed garlic and 1 tablespoon of the thyme and cook for another minute. Add the stock, bring to a boil, and cook for 8 minutes or until reduced slightly and the vegetables are tender. Gently stir in the lentils until heated through.

Stir in the remaining garlic and thyme and season with plenty of salt and black pepper—the stock should be slightly syrupy at this point. Combine the pasta with the lentil sauce in a large bowl, drizzle generously with extra-virgin olive oil, and serve with grated Parmesan, if desired.

Serves 4

# Fettucine with spinach and roasted tomatoes

6 Roma tomatoes
2 tablespoons butter
2 cloves garlic, crushed
1 onion, chopped
1 lb. spinach, trimmed
1 cup vegetable stock
½ cup thick cream
1 lb. fresh spinach fettucine
½ cup shaved Parmesan

Preheat the oven to 425°F. Cut the tomatoes in half lengthwise, then cut each half into 3 wedges. Place the wedges on a lightly greased baking tray and bake for 30–35 minutes or until softened and slightly golden. Meanwhile, heat the butter in a large frying pan. Add the garlic and onion and cook over medium heat for 5 minutes or until the onion is soft. Add the spinach, stock, and cream, increase the heat to high, and bring to a boil. Simmer for 5 minutes.

While the spinach mixture is cooking, cook the pasta in a large saucepan of boiling water until al dente. Drain and return to the saucepan. Remove the spinach from the heat and season well. Cool slightly, then process in a food processor until smooth. Toss through the pasta until well coated. Divide among serving bowls and top with the roasted tomatoes and Parmesan.

Serves 4–6

## Roasted tomatoes and ricotta tagliatelle

12 Roma tomatoes, halved
  lengthwise
½ cup olive oil
¼ teaspoon sugar
1 lb. fresh tagliatelle
2 cloves garlic, thinly sliced
1¼ cups fresh ricotta
½ cup fresh basil, shredded
½ cup grated Parmesan
2 teaspoons olive oil, extra

Preheat the oven to 400°F. Place the tomatoes cut-side up in a single layer in a large roasting pan and brush with 2 tablespoons oil. Sprinkle with the sugar, and season. Bake for 1 hour or until soft.

Meanwhile, cook the pasta in a large saucepan of lightly salted boiling water until al dente.

Heat the remaining oil in a frying pan, add the garlic, and cook for 1–2 minutes or until lightly golden. Drain the pasta, leaving it slightly wet, and place it in a large bowl with the tomatoes, garlic, oil from the pan, ricotta, basil, and Parmesan. Mix together well. Season with salt and freshly ground black pepper. Drizzle with the extra olive oil and serve.

Serves 4

Variation: Stir in ⅓ cup toasted pine nuts before serving.

## Linguine with ham, artichoke, and lemon sauce

1 lb. fresh linguine
1 tablespoon butter
2 large cloves garlic, chopped
$^2/_3$ cup marinated artichokes, drained
  and quartered
5 oz. sliced ham, cut into strips
1 $^1/_4$ cups cream
2 teaspoons coarsely grated
  lemon zest
$^1/_2$ cup fresh basil, torn
$^1/_3$ cup grated Parmesan

Cook the pasta in a large saucepan of boiling water until al dente. Drain, then return to the saucepan. Meanwhile, melt the butter in a large frying pan, add the garlic, and cook over medium heat for 1 minute or until fragrant. Add the artichokes and ham and cook for another 2 minutes.

Add the cream and lemon zest, reduce the heat, and simmer for 5 minutes, gently breaking up the artichokes with a wooden spoon. Pour the sauce over the pasta, then add the basil and Parmesan and toss well until the pasta is evenly coated. Divide among 4 serving plates and serve immediately.

Serves 4

## Wonton chicken ravioli with a Thai dressing

3/4 lb. ground chicken
2 scallions, finely chopped
3 kaffir lime leaves, very finely
    shredded
2 tablespoons sweet chili sauce
3 tablespoons chopped fresh
    cilantro leaves
1 1/2 teaspoons sesame oil
2 teaspoons grated lime zest
9-oz. packet wonton wrappers
1/2 cup fish sauce
2 tablespoons light brown sugar
1 tablespoon peanut oil
1 tablespoon lime juice
finely chopped fresh red chili,
    to garnish
chopped fresh cilantro leaves,
    to garnish

Combine the ground chicken, scallions, lime leaves, chili sauce, cilantro, sesame oil, and lime zest in a bowl.

Place a tablespoon of the mixture in the center of a wonton wrapper, brush the edges lightly with water, and top with another wrapper, pressing down around the edges to prevent the ravioli from opening during cooking. Repeat with the remaining filling and wrappers.

Cook the ravioli in batches in a large saucepan of boiling water for 5 minutes or until it is al dente and the ground chicken is cooked, then drain well and place on serving plates.

Combine the fish sauce, brown sugar, peanut oil, and lime juice in a bowl. Pour over the ravioli and garnish with the chopped chili and cilantro.

Serves 4 as an appetizer

## Bucatini with sausage and fennel seed

1 lb. good-quality Italian sausages
2 tablespoons olive oil
3 cloves garlic, chopped
1 teaspoon fennel seeds
$\frac{1}{2}$ teaspoon chili flakes
2 14-oz. cans crushed tomatoes
1 lb. bucatini pasta
1 teaspoon balsamic vinegar
$\frac{1}{4}$ cup loosely packed fresh basil, chopped

Heat a frying pan over high heat, add the sausages, and cook, turning frequently, for 8–10 minutes or until well browned and cooked through. Remove, cool slightly, and slice diagonally into $\frac{1}{2}$-inch pieces.

Heat the oil in a saucepan, add the garlic, and cook over medium heat for 1 minute. Add the fennel seeds and chili flakes and cook for another minute. Stir in the tomatoes and bring to a boil, then reduce the heat and simmer, covered, for 20 minutes. Meanwhile, cook the pasta in a large saucepan of boiling water until al dente. Drain and return to the saucepan to keep warm.

Add the sausages to the sauce and cook, uncovered, for 5 minutes to heat through. Stir in the balsamic vinegar and basil. Divide the pasta among 4 bowls, top with the sauce, and serve.

Serves 4

## Shrimp, tomato, and saffron pasta

¾ lb. tagliatelle
2 tablespoons olive oil
1 onion, diced
3 cloves garlic, chopped, with
  1 teaspoon salt
2 pinches of saffron threads
1 red pepper, diced
2 lbs. medium shrimp, peeled
  and deveined, with tails intact
1¼ cups whipping cream
¼ cup dry white wine
¼ cup fish or chicken stock
5 Roma tomatoes, peeled, seeded,
  and diced
1 cup roughly chopped fresh basil
2 tablespoons chopped fresh
  Italian parsley
⅓ cup Parmesan shavings

Cook the pasta in a large saucepan of boiling salted water until al dente. Drain and keep warm.

Meanwhile, heat the oil in a frying pan, add the onion, garlic, saffron, and red pepper, and stir over medium heat for 2 minutes before adding the shrimp. Cook for 2–3 minutes or until pink and cooked. Remove the shrimp with tongs and set aside.

Add the cream, wine, stock, and tomatoes to the pan and cook for 10 minutes or until reduced slightly. Add the herbs and the cooked shrimp. Season.

Toss with the pasta and serve topped with Parmesan shavings.

Serves 4–6

# Spaghettini with herbs, baby spinach, and garlic crumbs

3/4 lb. spaghettini
2 slices day-old crusty Italian bread, crusts removed
1/2 cup extra-virgin olive oil, plus extra for drizzling
4 cloves garlic, finely chopped
8 cups baby spinach leaves
1/2 cup chopped fresh Italian parsley
4 tablespoons chopped fresh basil
1 tablespoon fresh thyme leaves
1/3 cup shaved Parmesan

Cook the pasta in a large saucepan of boiling water until al dente. Drain, setting aside 1/2 cup of the pasta water. Return the pasta to the saucepan and keep warm.

To make the garlic bread crumbs, place the crustless bread in a food processor or blender and pulse until coarse bread crumbs form. Heat 1 tablespoon of the oil in a saucepan. Add the bread crumbs and half the garlic and toss for 2–3 minutes or until lightly golden. Remove, then wipe the saucepan clean with a paper towel.

Heat 2 tablespoons of the oil in the same saucepan. Add the spinach and remaining garlic, toss together for 1 minute, then add the herbs. Cook, tossing frequently, for another minute to wilt the herbs a little and to heat through. Toss the spinach mixture through the pasta with the remaining oil and pasta water. Divide among 4 serving bowls and sprinkle with the garlic crumbs. Serve hot sprinkled with Parmesan and drizzled with extra-virgin olive oil.

Serves 4

## Creamy pesto chicken penne

1 tablespoon vegetable oil
2 tablespoons butter
3/4 lb. skinless, boneless chicken breasts
8 thin asparagus spears, cut into 1 1/2-inch pieces
3 scallions, chopped
4 cloves garlic, crushed
1/2 cup whipping cream
1 1/4 cups sour cream
3/4 cup chicken stock
1 cup grated Parmesan
1/2 cup finely chopped fresh basil
2 tablespoons roasted pine nuts
3/4 lb. penne pasta
fresh basil leaves, to garnish

Heat the oil and half the butter in a large frying pan over high heat. Add the chicken and cook for 5 minutes on each side or until just cooked. Remove, cover, and cool, then cut into 1/2-inch slices.

Add the asparagus and scallions to the frying pan and cook for 2 minutes or until the asparagus is just tender. Remove. Wipe the pan with paper towels.

Reduce the heat to medium, add the remaining butter and the garlic, and cook for 2 minutes or until pale golden. Add the cream, sour cream, and stock, and simmer for 10 minutes or until reduced slightly. Add the Parmesan and basil and stir for 2 minutes or until the cheese has melted. Return the chicken and asparagus to the pan, add the pine nuts, and cook for 2 minutes to heat through. Season.

Meanwhile, cook the pasta in a large saucepan of lightly salted boiling water until al dente. Drain well. Combine the sauce and the pasta and garnish with basil leaves.

Serves 4

## Pasta with spinach, squash, and tomatoes

1½ lbs. butternut squash
2 tablespoons Parmesan-infused
  olive oil (see Notes)
16 unpeeled cloves garlic
½ lb. cherry tomatoes, halved
1 lb. orecchiette or penne pasta
4 cups spinach leaves
1½ cups marinated Persian feta
  (see Notes)
¼ cup sherry vinegar
2 tablespoons walnut oil

Preheat the oven to 400°F. Cut the squash into large cubes, place in a roasting pan, and drizzle with Parmesan oil. Roast for 30 minutes, then add the garlic and arrange the tomatoes in the pan. Place the vegetables in the oven and roast for 10–15 minutes or until cooked. Don't overcook the tomatoes or they will turn to mush.

Meanwhile, cook the pasta in a large saucepan of boiling water until al dente. Drain well.

Toss together the pasta, tomatoes, squash, garlic, and spinach in a large bowl. Drain the feta, setting aside ¼ cup of the marinade. Whisk the marinade, sherry vinegar, and walnut oil together. Pour over the pasta and sprinkle with pieces of the cheese.

Serves 4

Notes: Parmesan-infused olive oil is available at gourmet food stores and really adds depth of flavor. Persian feta is softer and creamier than other feta and is marinated in oil, herbs, and garlic.
Variation: Toss in 1 cup marinated Kalamata olives for extra flavor.

## Veal tortellini with creamy mushroom sauce

1 lb. veal tortellini
¼ cup olive oil
1¼ lbs. portobello mushrooms,
   thinly sliced
2 cloves garlic, crushed
½ cup dry white wine
1¼ cups whipping cream
pinch of ground nutmeg
3 tablespoons finely chopped
   fresh Italian parsley
⅓ cup grated Parmesan

Cook the pasta in a large saucepan of boiling water until al dente. Drain. Meanwhile, heat the oil in a frying pan over medium heat. Add the mushrooms and cook, stirring occasionally, for 5 minutes or until softened. Add the garlic and cook for 1 minute, then stir in the wine and cook for 5 minutes or until the liquid has reduced by half.

Combine the cream, nutmeg, and parsley, add to the sauce, and cook for 3–5 minutes or until the sauce thickens slightly. Season. Divide the tortellini among 4 serving plates and spoon on the mushroom sauce. Sprinkle with Parmesan and serve.

Serves 4

# Sweet potato gnocchi with wilted greens

1 lb. russet potatoes, chopped
1/2 lb. orange sweet potatoes, chopped
1 egg yolk
2 tablespoons milk
1/4 teaspoon ground nutmeg
1 1/4 cups all-purpose flour
1 tablespoon olive oil
4 bacon slices, thinly sliced
1 small onion, chopped
1/3 cup sweet sherry
1 lb. spinach
2 tablespoons butter
2 tablespoons roasted pine nuts

Preheat the oven to 425°F. Bake the potatoes and sweet potatoes in a roasting pan for 40–60 minutes or until soft. Cut in half and leave for 10 minutes. While still warm, press through a strainer into a large bowl. Add the egg yolk and milk, then the nutmeg, 1 cup flour, and 1 1/4 teaspoons salt, and mix well to combine.

Lightly knead the mixture until it is smooth, adding more flour if it becomes sticky. Roll into 3/4-inch cylinders, then cut diagonally into 3/4-inch pieces. Indent on one side with a fork.

Heat the oil in a large frying pan, add the bacon and onion, and cook over medium heat for 5 minutes or until the onion starts to become golden. Add the sherry, stir well, and cook for 2 minutes or until reduced slightly. Add the spinach and cook, stirring, for 2 minutes or until wilted but still bright green. Stir in the butter and season. Keep warm.

Cook the gnocchi in boiling water in batches for 2–3 minutes or until they rise to the surface. Drain and toss through the sauce. Sprinkle the pine nuts over the top.

Serves 4

# Spaghetti Bolognese

¼ cup butter
1 onion, finely chopped
2 cloves garlic, crushed
1 celery stalk, finely chopped
1 carrot, diced
2-oz. piece pancetta, diced
1 lb. ground beef
1 tablespoon chopped fresh oregano
1 cup red wine
2 cups beef stock
2 tablespoons tomato paste
2 13-oz. cans crushed tomatoes
¾ lb. spaghetti
3 tablespoons grated Parmesan

Melt the butter in a large saucepan, add the onion, and cook over medium heat for 2–3 minutes or until it starts to soften. Add the garlic, celery, and carrot, and cook, stirring, over low heat for 5 minutes. Increase the heat to high, add the pancetta, beef, and oregano, and cook for 4–5 minutes or until browned. Use a fork to break up any lumps.

Pour in the wine, reduce the heat, and simmer for 4–5 minutes or until it is absorbed. Add the stock, tomato paste, and tomatoes, and season well. Cover with a lid and simmer for 1½ hours, stirring occasionally to prevent the sauce from catching on the bottom of the saucepan. Uncover and simmer for another hour, stirring occasionally.

Cook the spaghetti in a large saucepan of boiling water until al dente. Drain, divide among 4 serving plates, and top with the sauce. Sprinkle with the Parmesan and serve.

Serves 4

# Cresti di gallo with creamy tomato and bacon sauce

3/4 lb. cresti di gallo, rotelle, or cotelli pasta
1 tablespoon olive oil
6 oz. bacon
1 lb. Roma tomatoes, roughly chopped
1/2 cup whipping cream
2 tablespoons sun-dried tomato pesto
2 tablespoons finely chopped fresh Italian parsley
1/2 cup finely grated Parmesan

Cook the pasta in a large saucepan of boiling water until al dente. Drain well and return to the saucepan. Meanwhile, heat the oil in a frying pan, add the bacon, and cook over high heat for 2 minutes or until starting to brown. Reduce the heat to medium, add the tomatoes, and cook, stirring frequently, for 2 minutes or until the tomatoes have softened but still hold their shape.

Add the cream and tomato pesto and stir until heated through. Remove from the heat, add the parsley, then toss the sauce through the pasta with the grated Parmesan.

Serves 4

## Roast squash sauce on pappardelle

3 lbs. butternut squash, cut
  into ¾-inch pieces
4 cloves garlic, crushed
3 teaspoons fresh thyme leaves
½ cup olive oil
1 lb. pappardelle pasta
2 tablespoons cream
¾ cup hot chicken stock
⅓ cup shaved Parmesan

Preheat the oven to 400°F. Place the squash, garlic, thyme, and ¼ cup of the olive oil in a bowl and toss together. Season with salt, transfer to a baking tray, and cook for 30 minutes or until tender and golden. Meanwhile, cook the pasta in a large saucepan of boiling water until al dente. Drain and return to the saucepan. Toss through the remaining oil and keep warm.

Place the cooked squash and the cream in a food processor or blender and process until smooth. Add the hot stock and process until smooth and combined. Season with salt and cracked black pepper and gently toss through the warm pasta. Divide among 4 serving plates, sprinkle with Parmesan and extra thyme, if desired, and serve immediately.

Serves 4

Note: The sauce becomes too thick if allowed to rest, so serve it as soon as possible.

## Tagliatelle with chicken, herbs, and mushrooms

2 tablespoons olive oil
3/4 lb. chicken tenderloins, cut
  into 3/4-inch pieces
1 tablespoon butter
3/4 lb. mushrooms, sliced
2 cloves garlic, finely chopped
1/2 cup dry white wine
3/4 cup whipping cream
3/4 lb. tagliatelle
1 teaspoon finely grated lemon zest
2 tablespoons lemon juice
2 tablespoons chopped fresh
  marjoram
2 tablespoons chopped fresh parsley
1 cup grated Parmesan

Heat 1 tablespoon oil in a large frying pan, add the chicken, and cook over medium heat for 3–4 minutes or until lightly browned. Remove.

Heat the butter and remaining oil, add the mushrooms, and cook, stirring, over high heat for 3 minutes. Add the garlic and cook for another 2 minutes.

Stir in the wine, reduce the heat, and simmer for 5 minutes or until nearly evaporated. Stir in the whipping cream and chicken and simmer for 5 minutes or until thickened.

Meanwhile, cook the tagliatelle in lightly salted boiling water until al dente. Drain. Keep warm.

Stir the lemon zest and juice, marjoram, parsley, and 2 tablespoons Parmesan into the sauce. Season, combine with the pasta, and serve with the remaining Parmesan.

Serves 4

## Spaghetti with smoked tuna and olives

1³/₄ lbs. vine-ripened tomatoes
³/₄ lb. spaghetti
3 4-oz. cans smoked tuna slices
  in oil
1 red onion, chopped
2 cloves garlic, crushed
1 teaspoon sugar
1 cup black olives
2 tablespoons chopped fresh basil
¹/₂ cup feta, crumbled

Score a cross in the bottom of each tomato. Place the tomatoes in a bowl of boiling water for 1 minute, then plunge into cold water and peel the skin away from the cross. Cut in half and remove the seeds with a teaspoon. Roughly chop the flesh. Cook the pasta in a large saucepan of boiling water until al dente. Drain and keep warm.

Drain the oil from the tuna slices, saving 1 tablespoon. Heat the tuna oil in a large saucepan, add the onion, and cook over low heat for 3–4 minutes or until soft but not brown. Add the garlic and cook for another minute, then add the chopped tomatoes and sugar. Cook over medium heat for 8–10 minutes or until pulpy.

Add the tuna slices, olives, and chopped basil, stir well, and cook for 2 minutes or until warmed through. Toss through the spaghetti and season with salt and cracked black pepper. Sprinkle with crumbled feta and serve immediately.

Serves 4

# Rice

## Risi e bisi

5 cups chicken stock
bouquet garni (1 sprig fresh thyme,
  1 bay leaf, 2 stalks fresh Italian
  parsley)
2 tablespoons olive oil
1 onion, chopped
1/2 celery stalk, chopped
2 oz. pancetta, chopped
1/2 lb. arborio rice
2 cups frozen baby peas
1/4 cup unsalted butter
3/4 cup grated Parmesan
shaved Parmesan, to serve

Place the stock and bouquet garni in a large saucepan with 3 cups water. Bring to a boil, then reduce the heat and simmer.

Heat the oil in a large frying pan, add the onion, celery, and pancetta, and cook for 3–5 minutes or until the onion is soft. Add the rice and stir for 1 minute or until coated.

Remove the bouquet garni and add 1/2 cup hot stock to the rice, stirring constantly until all the stock is absorbed. Add another 1/2 cup stock and stir until all the stock is absorbed. Add the peas. Continue adding stock, 1/2 cup at a time, stirring, for 20–25 minutes or until the rice is tender. The texture should be a little wetter than risotto, but not too soupy. Remove from the heat and stir in the butter and grated Parmesan. Season. Garnish with shaved Parmesan.

Serves 4

# Chicken and mushroom risotto

5 cups vegetable or chicken stock
2 tablespoons olive oil
10 oz. skinless, boneless chicken
  breasts, cut into ½-inch-wide strips
½ lb. small button mushrooms,
  halved
pinch nutmeg
2 cloves garlic, crushed
1 tablespoon butter
1 small onion, finely chopped
¾ lb. arborio rice
⅔ cup dry white wine
3 tablespoons sour cream
3 tablespoons finely chopped fresh
  Italian parsley
½ cup freshly grated Parmesan

Bring the stock to a boil, reduce the heat, and keep at a simmer. Heat the oil in a large saucepan. Cook the chicken over high heat for 3–4 minutes or until golden brown. Add the mushrooms and cook for 1–2 minutes more or until starting to brown. Stir in the nutmeg and garlic and season with salt and pepper. Cook for 30 seconds, then remove from the saucepan and set aside.

Melt the butter in the same saucepan and cook the onion over low heat for 5–6 minutes. Add the rice, stir to coat, then add the wine. Once the wine is absorbed, reduce the heat and add ½ cup of the stock. When it is absorbed, add another ½ cup. Continue adding stock for 20–25 minutes or until all the stock has been used and the rice is creamy. Add the mushrooms and the chicken with the remainder of the stock.

Remove the saucepan from the heat and stir in the sour cream, parsley, and Parmesan. Check the seasoning, then cover and allow to rest for 2 minutes before serving.

Serves 4

# Asparagus and pistachio risotto

4 cups vegetable stock
1 cup white wine
1/3 cup extra-virgin olive oil
1 red onion, finely chopped
2 cups arborio rice
3/4 lb. asparagus spears, trimmed
  and cut into 1-inch pieces
1/2 cup whipping cream
1 cup grated Parmesan
1/2 cup shelled pistachio nuts, roasted
  and roughly chopped

Heat the stock and wine in a large saucepan, bring to a boil, then reduce the heat, cover, and keep at a low simmer.

Heat the oil in another saucepan. Add the onion and cook over medium heat for 3 minutes or until soft. Add the rice and stir for 1 minute or until the rice is translucent.

Add 1/2 cup hot stock, stirring constantly over medium heat until the liquid is absorbed. Continue adding stock, 1/2 cup at a time, stirring constantly for 20–25 minutes or until all the stock is absorbed and the rice is tender and creamy. Add the asparagus pieces during the final 5 minutes of cooking. Remove from the heat.

Allow to rest for 2 minutes, stir in the cream and Parmesan, and season to taste with salt and black pepper. Serve sprinkled with pistachios.

Serves 4–6

# Chicken gumbo

2 tablespoons butter
2 bacon slices
1 small onion, chopped
1 small green pepper, diced
2 cloves garlic, chopped
1/4 teaspoon cayenne pepper
1 1/4 lbs. skinless, boneless chicken
  breasts, cubed
1/4 teaspoon saffron threads, soaked
  in 2 tablespoons warm water
1 tablespoon brandy
1 tablespoon tomato paste
2 tablespoons all-purpose flour
4 cups chicken stock
3/4 cup basmati rice
1 tablespoon olive oil
3/4 lb. raw small shrimp, peeled,
  deveined, with tails intact
3/4 lb. okra, thickly sliced
2 tablespoons whipping cream
3 tablespoons chopped fresh
  Italian parsley
1/2 teaspoon hot pepper sauce

Melt the butter in a large saucepan
over medium heat, add the bacon,
onion, green pepper, garlic, cayenne,
and chicken, and cook, stirring,
for 5–8 minutes or until light golden.
Stir in the saffron and soaking liquid,
the brandy, tomato paste, and flour,
and cook, stirring constantly, for
3 minutes.

Gradually add the stock and bring
to a boil. Add the rice, then reduce
the heat to low and simmer gently
for 10 minutes.

Meanwhile, heat the olive oil in a
separate saucepan, add the shrimp
and okra, and toss quickly together
for 1–2 minutes or until the shrimp
change color. Add to the gumbo,
then stir in the cream, parsley, and
hot pepper sauce, and heat for
1–2 minutes. Serve in deep bowls
with corn bread.

Serves 4–6

## Chicken and mushroom pilaf

1½ cups basmati rice
2 tablespoons vegetable oil
1 large onion, chopped
3–4 cloves garlic, crushed
1 tablespoon finely chopped
  fresh ginger
1 lb. chicken tenderloins, trimmed
  and cut into small pieces
¾ lb. portobello mushrooms, sliced
¾ cup slivered almonds, toasted
1½–2 teaspoons garam masala,
  dry roasted
½ cup plain yogurt
1 tablespoon finely chopped fresh
  cilantro leaves
fresh cilantro leaves, extra, to garnish

Rinse the rice under cold water until the water runs clear. Drain and leave for 30 minutes. Heat the oil in a large saucepan and stir in the onion, garlic, and ginger. Reduce the heat to medium and cook, covered, for 5 minutes or until the onion has browned. Increase the heat to high, add the chicken, and cook, stirring, for 3–4 minutes or until the chicken is lightly browned. Stir in the sliced mushrooms, almonds, and garam masala. Cook, covered, for another 3 minutes or until the mushrooms are soft. Uncover and cook without stirring for 2 minutes or until the liquid has evaporated.

Remove the chicken from the pan. Add the rice and stir for 30 seconds or until well-coated in the mushroom and onion mixture. Pour in 1½ cups water and bring to a boil, stirring frequently, for 2 minutes or until most of the water evaporates. Return the chicken to the pan. Cover, reduce the heat to low, and steam for 15 minutes or until the rice is cooked.

Combine the yogurt and chopped cilantro. Fluff the rice with a fork and divide among serving bowls. Top with a dollop of the yogurt mixture and garnish with cilantro leaves.

Serves 4–6

# Paella

1 lb. mussels
¼ cup olive oil
1¼ lbs. chicken drumettes or
  skinless, boneless thighs, halved
1 onion, chopped
2 large cloves garlic, chopped
3 vine-ripened tomatoes, peeled,
  seeded, and finely chopped
1 small red pepper, diced
1 small green pepper, diced
¼ teaspoon chili flakes
1 teaspoon paprika
¼ teaspoon saffron threads, soaked
  in ¼ cup warm water
1⅓ cups short-grain rice
4 cups vegetable stock
12 medium shrimp, peeled, deveined,
  with tails intact
1 cup peas
¼ cup dry sherry
½ cup chopped fresh Italian parsley
1 lemon, cut into wedges

Scrub the mussels and remove the beards. Discard any open mussels that don't close when tapped.

Heat 2 tablespoons oil in a large frying pan, add the chicken, and cook over medium heat for 5–7 minutes or until browned. Remove. Add the remaining oil to the pan, then add the onion, garlic, and tomatoes, and cook over low heat for 5 minutes or until soft. Do not brown. Add the peppers and cook for 1 minute, then stir in the chili flakes, paprika, and saffron and its soaking liquid. Pour in the rice and return the chicken to the pan. Add the stock, bring to a boil, then reduce the heat and simmer for 10 minutes.

Stir in the shrimp, peas, sherry, and mussels. Cover for 2 minutes or until the mussels open. Discard any that do not open. Stir for 2 minutes or until the shrimp are pink and cooked through. Stir in the parsley. Serve immediately with the lemon wedges.

Serves 4

## Risotto with scallops and minted peas

4 cups chicken, fish, or vegetable
 stock
2³/₄ cups fresh or frozen baby peas
2 tablespoons light sour cream
2 tablespoons finely shredded fresh
 mint
1 tablespoon olive oil
1 small onion, finely chopped
2 cloves garlic, finely chopped
²/₃ cup arborio rice
16 large scallops, without roe
1 tablespoon grated fresh Parmesan
4 fresh mint leaves, to garnish
lemon wedges, to serve

Bring the stock to a boil and add
the peas. Simmer for 1–2 minutes
or until the peas are tender, then
remove, keeping the stock at a
low simmer. Blend 1³/₄ cups of the
peas with the sour cream in a food
processor until smooth. Season,
then stir in 1 tablespoon of the mint.

Place the oil in a shallow saucepan
and cook the onion over low heat
for 4–5 minutes or until soft. Add
the garlic and cook for 30 seconds.
Stir in the rice to coat. Increase the
heat to medium.

Add 1 cup stock to the rice mixture
and cook, stirring constantly, until
the liquid has evaporated. Add
the stock, ¹/₂ cup at a time, until
the rice is tender and creamy. This
will take approximately 20 minutes.
Meanwhile, season the scallops
and heat a griddle or skillet. Add
the scallops and sear on both sides
until cooked through.

Fold the pea purée through the
risotto with the peas and Parmesan.
Divide the risotto among the serving
bowls and top with the scallops.
Sprinkle with the remaining mint,
garnish with a mint leaf, and serve
with a wedge of lemon.

Serves 4–6

# Green pilaf with cashews

4 cups baby spinach leaves
2/3 cup cashew nuts, chopped
2 tablespoons olive oil
6 scallions, chopped
1½ cups long-grain brown rice
2 cloves garlic, finely chopped
1 teaspoon fennel seeds
2 tablespoons lemon juice
2½ cups vegetable stock
3 tablespoons chopped fresh mint
3 tablespoons chopped fresh
  Italian parsley

Preheat the oven to 350°F. Shred the spinach into ½-inch pieces.

Place the cashews on a baking tray and roast for 5–10 minutes or until golden brown—make sure they don't burn.

Heat the oil in a large frying pan and cook the scallions over medium heat for 2 minutes or until soft. Add the rice, garlic, and fennel seeds, and cook, stirring frequently, for 1–2 minutes or until the rice is evenly coated. Increase the heat to high, add the lemon juice, stock, and 1 teaspoon salt, and bring to a boil. Reduce the heat to low, cover, and cook for 45 minutes without lifting the lid.

Remove from the heat and sprinkle with the spinach and herbs. Allow to rest, covered, for 8 minutes, then fork the spinach and herbs through the rice. Season. Serve sprinkled with cashews.

Serves 6

## Lemon and zucchini risotto

5 cups hot vegetable or chicken
stock
2 tablespoons olive oil
1 onion, finely chopped
1²/₃ cups arborio rice
¹/₃ cup dry sherry
3 teaspoons grated lemon zest
2 tablespoons lemon juice
³/₄ lb. zucchini, diced
2 tablespoons chopped fresh
Italian parsley
¹/₂ cup freshly grated Parmesan
lemon zest, to garnish

Place the stock in a large saucepan,
bring to a boil, then reduce the heat,
cover, and keep at a low simmer.

Heat the oil in a large saucepan, add
the onion, and cook over medium
heat for 5 minutes or until softened.
Reduce the heat, stir in the rice, and
cook for 1 minute, stirring constantly.

Add ¹/₂ cup hot stock, stirring until
all the stock is absorbed. Continue
adding the stock, ¹/₂ cup at a time,
stirring constantly, for 20 minutes
or until all the liquid is absorbed.
If the risotto gets too dry, add a
little extra stock or water. Stir in
the sherry, lemon zest, lemon juice,
and zucchini. Cook over low heat for
another 5 minutes or until the risotto
is tender with a slight bite to the
inside of the grain. Season with
salt and freshly ground black pepper
and stir in the parsley and half the
Parmesan. Garnish with the lemon
zest and remaining Parmesan.

Serves 4

# Chicken and pork paella

¼ cup olive oil
1 large red pepper, seeded and
cut into ¼-inch strips
1¼ lbs. skinless, boneless chicken
thighs, cut into 1-inch cubes
6 oz. chorizo sausage, cut into
1-inch slices
2 cups mushrooms, thinly sliced
3 cloves garlic, crushed
1 tablespoon lemon zest
1½ lbs. tomatoes, roughly chopped
1½ cups green beans, cut into
1-inch pieces
1 tablespoon chopped fresh
rosemary
2 tablespoons chopped fresh
Italian parsley
¼ teaspoon saffron threads,
dissolved in ¼ cup hot water
2 cups short-grain rice
3 cups hot chicken stock
6 lemon wedges

Heat the olive oil in a large, deep frying pan or paella pan over medium heat. Add the pepper and cook for 6 minutes or until softened. Remove from the pan. Add the chicken to the pan and cook for 10 minutes or until brown on all sides. Remove. Add the sausage to the pan and cook for 5 minutes or until golden on all sides. Remove.

Add the mushrooms, garlic, and lemon zest, and cook over medium heat for 5 minutes. Stir in the tomatoes and pepper and cook for another 5 minutes or until the tomatoes are soft.

Add the beans, rosemary, parsley, saffron mixture, rice, chicken, and sausage. Stir briefly and add the stock. Do not stir. Reduce the heat and simmer for 30 minutes. Remove from the heat, cover, and allow to rest for 10 minutes. Serve with lemon wedges.

Serves 6

Note: Paellas are not stirred to the bottom of the pan during cooking, as it is hoped that a thin crust of crispy rice—considered one of the best parts of the paella—will form. For this reason, it is important not to use a nonstick frying pan.

## Asian barley pilaf

1/2 oz. dried sliced mushrooms
2 cups vegetable stock
1/2 cup dry sherry
1 tablespoon vegetable oil
3 large French shallots, thinly sliced
2 large cloves garlic, crushed
1 tablespoon grated fresh ginger
1 teaspoon Szechuan peppercorns,
  crushed
1 1/2 cups pearl barley
1 lb. choy sum, cut into 2-inch pieces
3 teaspoons kecap manis
  (sweet soy sauce)
1 teaspoon sesame oil

Place the mushrooms in a bowl and cover with boiling water, then leave for 15 minutes. Strain, setting aside 1/2 cup of the liquid.

Bring the stock and sherry to a boil in a saucepan, then reduce the heat, cover, and simmer until needed.

Heat the oil in a large saucepan and cook the shallots over medium heat for 2–3 minutes or until soft. Add the garlic, ginger, and peppercorns, and cook for 1 minute. Add the barley and mushrooms and mix well. Stir in the stock and mushroom liquid, then reduce the heat and simmer, covered, for 25 minutes or until all of the liquid evaporates.

Meanwhile, steam the choy sum until it is wilted. Add to the barley mixture. Stir in the kecap manis and sesame oil before serving.

Serves 4

## Squash risotto

1 1/4 lbs. squash, cut into
  1/2-inch cubes
3 tablespoons olive oil
2 cups vegetable stock
1 onion, finely chopped
2 cloves garlic, finely chopped
1 tablespoon chopped fresh
  rosemary
2 cups arborio rice
1/2 cup white wine
2 tablespoons butter
1/3 cup grated Parmesan
3 tablespoons finely chopped fresh
  Italian parsley

Preheat the oven to 400°F. Toss the pieces of squash in 2 tablespoons of the oil, place in a baking dish, and roast for 30 minutes or until tender and golden. Turn the squash pieces halfway through the cooking time.

Heat the stock and 3 cups water in a saucepan, cover, and keep at a low simmer.

Heat the remaining oil in a large saucepan and cook the onion, garlic, and rosemary, stirring, over low heat for 5 minutes or until the onion is cooked but not browned. Add the rice and stir to coat. Stir in the wine for 2–3 minutes or until absorbed.

Add 1/2 cup stock, stirring constantly over medium heat until all the liquid is absorbed. Continue adding the stock 1/2 cup at a time, stirring constantly, for 20 minutes or until all the stock is absorbed and the rice is tender and creamy. Season to taste with salt and black pepper and stir in the squash, butter, Parmesan, and parsley. Serve immediately.

Serves 4–6

# Shrimp pilaf

2 cups basmati rice
1/4 cup butter
1 onion, finely chopped
2 cloves garlic, finely chopped
1/2 x 1 1/2-inch piece fresh ginger,
   peeled and grated
1 fresh green chili, finely chopped
3 teaspoons cilantro seeds
1 teaspoon ground turmeric
2 cardamom pods, cracked
2 lbs. medium shrimp, peeled
   and deveined, with tails intact
1/2 cup cashew nuts (unroasted)
1/3 cup lemon juice
1/2 cup chopped fresh cilantro leaves

Rinse the rice under cold water until the water runs clear. Drain well. Melt 2 tablespoons butter over low heat in a large saucepan; add the onion and cook for 3 minutes or until soft. Add the garlic, ginger, chili, cilantro seeds, and turmeric, and cook for 2 minutes.

Add the rice to the saucepan and cook for 1 minute, then add the cardamom pods and 4 cups water. Bring to a boil, then reduce the heat and simmer, covered, for 10 minutes or until the rice is tender. Remove from the heat and allow to steam, covered, for 5 minutes.

Melt the remaining butter in a frying pan and cook the shrimp and cashew nuts over high heat for 3–4 minutes or until the shrimp are pink and cooked through. Add both to the pan with the rice, then add the lemon juice and cilantro, and stir everything together. Season to taste with salt and pepper, and serve.

Serves 4–6

## Mushroom risotto

6 cups vegetable stock
2 cups white wine
2 tablespoons olive oil
1/4 cup butter
2 leeks, thinly sliced
2 lbs. flat mushrooms, sliced
1 lb. arborio rice
3/4 cup grated Parmesan
3 tablespoons chopped fresh
   Italian parsley
balsamic vinegar, to serve
shaved Parmesan, to garnish
fresh Italian parsley, to garnish

Place the stock and wine in a large saucepan, bring to a boil, then reduce the heat to low, cover, and keep at a low simmer.

Meanwhile, heat the oil and butter in a large saucepan. Add the leeks and cook over medium heat for 5 minutes or until soft and golden. Add the mushrooms and cook for 5 minutes or until tender. Add the rice and stir for 1 minute or until the rice is translucent.

Add 1/2 cup hot stock, stirring constantly, over medium heat until the liquid is absorbed. Continue adding more stock, 1/2 cup at a time, stirring constantly between additions, for 20–25 minutes or until all the stock is absorbed and the rice is tender and creamy in texture.

Stir in the Parmesan and chopped parsley and heat for 1 minute or until all the cheese is melted. Serve drizzled with balsamic vinegar, topped with Parmesan shavings, and garnished with the parsley.

Serves 4

# Chicken and asparagus risotto

6 cups chicken stock
1 cup dry white wine
6 whole black peppercorns
2 bay leaves
1 tablespoon olive oil
2 tablespoons butter
1¼ lbs. skinless, boneless chicken
  breasts, cut into ¾-inch cubes
1 leek, sliced
2 cloves garlic, crushed
2 cups arborio rice
12 asparagus spears, cut into
  1-inch pieces
½ cup grated Parmesan
2 tablespoons lemon juice
3 tablespoons chopped fresh
  Italian parsley
shaved Parmesan, to garnish

Place the stock, wine, peppercorns, and bay leaves in a saucepan and simmer for 5 minutes. Strain, return to the saucepan, and keep at a low simmer.

Heat the oil and half the butter in a saucepan, add the chicken, and cook over medium heat for 5 minutes or until golden. Remove. Add the leek and garlic and cook for 5 minutes or until softened.

Add the rice and stir for 1 minute to coat. Add ½ cup stock, stirring until absorbed. Continue adding stock, ½ cup at a time, stirring constantly for 20–25 minutes, until the stock is absorbed and the rice is tender. Add the asparagus and chicken during the last 5 minutes.

When the chicken is cooked through, stir in the Parmesan, juice, parsley, and remaining butter. Season, then garnish with the shaved Parmesan.

Serves 4

## Rice and red lentil pilaf

¼ cup vegetable oil
1 onion, chopped
3 cloves garlic, chopped
1 cup basmati rice
1 cup red lentils
3 cups hot vegetable stock
scallions, thinly sliced diagonally,
  to garnish

*Garam masala*
1 tablespoon cilantro seeds
1 tablespoon cardamom pods
1 tablespoon cumin seeds
1 teaspoon whole black peppercorns
1 teaspoon whole cloves
1 small cinnamon stick, crushed

To make the garam masala, place all the spices in a dry frying pan and shake over medium heat for 1 minute or until fragrant. Blend to a fine powder in a spice grinder or blender.

Heat the oil in a large saucepan. Add the onion, garlic, and 3 teaspoons garam masala. Cook over medium heat for 3 minutes or until the onion is soft.

Stir in the rice and lentils and cook for 2 minutes. Add the hot stock and stir well. Slowly bring to a boil, then reduce the heat and simmer, covered, for 15–20 minutes or until the rice is cooked and all the stock has been absorbed. Gently fluff the rice with a fork. Garnish with scallions.

Serves 4–6

Note: You can use store-bought garam masala instead of making it.

## Chinese fried rice

¼ cup vegetable oil
2 eggs, lightly beaten
1 carrot, thinly sliced
1 red pepper, diced
6 fresh baby corn, sliced
2 cloves garlic, crushed
3½ oz. sausages, sliced diagonally
½ cup frozen peas
3 lbs. cooked long-grain rice, cooled
3 scallions, thinly sliced
3½ tablespoons soy sauce
2 teaspoons sugar
2 teaspoons sesame oil

Heat a wok or large frying pan over high heat, add 1 tablespoon of the oil, and swirl to coat. Add the eggs and swirl to distribute evenly. Cook for 1–2 minutes or until golden, then turn and cook the other side. Remove the omelet, leave until cool enough to handle, then roll up and slice thinly.

Heat the remaining oil over high heat, add the carrot, and stir-fry for 1 minute, then add the red pepper and cook for another minute. Finally, add the corn, garlic, sausages, and peas, and stir-fry for 1 minute.

Add the rice, scallions, and omelet, and mix, separating the rice grains. Stir over medium heat for 3 minutes or until the rice is warmed through. Stir in the soy sauce, sugar, and sesame oil, and toss. Serve hot.

Serves 4–6

Variation: Instead of sausage, try barbecued pork, sliced ham, or shrimp.

## Sweet potato and sage risotto

8 slices prosciutto
1/3 cup extra-virgin olive oil
1 red onion, cut into thin wedges
1 1/4 lbs. orange sweet potato, peeled
  and cut into 1-inch cubes
2 cups arborio rice
5 cups hot chicken stock
3/4 cup shredded Parmesan
3 tablespoons shredded fresh sage

Place the prosciutto slices on a baking tray and cook under a hot broiler for 1–2 minutes each side or until crispy.

Heat 1/4 cup oil in a large saucepan, add the onion, and cook over medium heat for 2–3 minutes or until softened. Add the sweet potato and rice and stir through until well-coated in the oil.

Add 1/2 cup hot chicken stock, stirring constantly over medium heat until the liquid is absorbed. Continue adding more stock, 1/2 cup at a time, stirring constantly, for 20–25 minutes or until all the stock is absorbed and the rice is tender and creamy. Stir in the shredded Parmesan and 2 tablespoons of the sage. Season. Spoon into 4 bowls and drizzle with the remaining oil. Break the prosciutto into pieces and sprinkle over the top with the remaining sage. Top with shaved Parmesan, if desired. Serve immediately.

Serves 4

# Jambalaya

1 tablespoon olive oil
2 skinless, boneless chicken breasts,
  cut into $1/2$ x $2^1/2$-inch strips
1 red onion, sliced
3 bacon slices, chopped
2 chorizo sausages, cut into
  $1/2$-inch diagonal slices
1 small red pepper, sliced
1 small green pepper, sliced
2 cloves garlic, finely chopped
1–2 teaspoons seeded, finely
  chopped fresh jalapeño chili
1 teaspoon smoked paprika
3 teaspoons Cajun spice mix
2 cups long-grain rice, washed
1 cup beer
4 vine-ripened tomatoes, peeled
  and quartered
3 cups chicken stock
$1/2$ teaspoon saffron threads, soaked
  in 1 tablespoon warm water
16 medium shrimp, peeled, deveined,
  with tails intact

Heat the oil in a large saucepan. Cook the chicken in batches over medium heat for 4 minutes or until lightly browned. Remove.

Cook the onion for 3 minutes, then add the bacon and sausage and cook for 4–5 minutes or until browned. Add the peppers and cook for 2 minutes, then add the garlic, chili, paprika, and Cajun spice mix, and cook for another 2 minutes.

Add the rice and stir to coat. Add the beer and stir for 30 seconds to remove any sediment stuck to the saucepan. Stir in the tomatoes, stock, saffron, and soaking liquid. Bring to a boil, reduce the heat, and simmer, covered, for 10–12 minutes.

Add the shrimp and chicken, stir to prevent from sticking, and cook, covered, for 3–5 minutes or until the rice is creamy and tender.

Serves 6

## Baked shrimp risotto with Thai flavors

1 1/4 cups stock (fish, chicken,
  or vegetable)
1 lemongrass stalk, lightly smashed
4 fresh kaffir lime leaves, finely
  shredded
2 tablespoons vegetable oil
1 small red onion, thinly sliced
1 1/2–2 tablespoons good-quality
  store-bought Thai red curry paste
1 1/2 cups arborio rice
1 1/4 cups coconut cream
1 1/4 lbs. shrimp, peeled and deveined,
  with tails intact

Preheat the oven to 350°F. Pour the stock into a saucepan, then add the lemongrass and half of the kaffir lime leaves. Bring to a boil, then reduce the heat and simmer, covered, for 10 minutes.

Heat the oil in a flameproof casserole dish with a lid. Add the onion and cook over medium–low heat for 4–5 minutes or until soft but not browned. Stir in the curry paste and cook for another minute or until fragrant. Stir in the rice until well-coated. Strain the stock into the rice, then add the coconut cream. Cover and bake for 15 minutes.

Remove from the oven, stir the risotto well, then bake for another 10–15 minutes. Add the shrimp and mix them well into the rice—if the mixture looks a little dry, add 1/2 cup stock or water. Bake for another 10–15 minutes or until the shrimp are cooked through and the rice is tender. Serve the risotto in bowls, garnished with the remaining shredded lime leaves.

Serves 4

Wok

# Sweet chili shrimp

2 lbs. medium shrimp
2 tablespoons peanut oil
½ x 1¼-inch piece fresh ginger,
  julienned
2 cloves garlic, finely chopped
5 scallions, cut into 1-inch pieces
⅓ cup chili garlic sauce
2 tablespoons tomato sauce
2 tablespoons Chinese rice wine
  (see Notes)
1 tablespoon Chinese black vinegar
  or rice vinegar (see Notes)
1 tablespoon soy sauce
1 tablespoon light brown sugar
1 teaspoon cornstarch, mixed with
  ½ cup water
finely chopped scallions, to garnish

Peel and devein the shrimp, leaving the tails intact. Heat a wok until very hot, then add the oil and swirl to coat the side. Heat over high heat until smoking, then quickly add the ginger, garlic, and scallions, and stir-fry for 1 minute. Add the shrimp and cook for 2 minutes or until they are just pink and starting to curl. Remove the shrimp from the wok with tongs or a slotted spoon.

Put the chili garlic sauce, tomato sauce, rice wine, vinegar, soy sauce, brown sugar, and cornstarch paste in a small pitcher and whisk together. Pour the sauce into the wok and cook, stirring, for 1–2 minutes or until it thickens slightly. Return the shrimp to the wok for 1–2 minutes or until heated and cooked through. Garnish with the finely chopped scallions. Serve immediately with rice noodles or thin egg noodles.

Serves 4

Notes: Chinese rice wine has a rich, sweetish taste. Use dry sherry if unavailable. Chinese black vinegar is made from rice and has a sweet, mild taste. It is available in Asian food stores.

## Chicken with Thai basil, chilies, and cashews

1½ lbs. skinless, boneless chicken
  breasts or thighs, cut into strips
2 lemongrass stalks, white part only,
  finely chopped
3 small fresh red chilies, seeded and
  finely chopped
4 cloves garlic, crushed
1 tablespoon finely chopped fresh
  ginger
2 fresh cilantro roots, finely chopped
2 tablespoons vegetable oil
⅔ cup cashews
1½ tablespoons lime juice
2 tablespoons fish sauce
1½ tablespoons light brown sugar
2 cups lightly packed fresh Thai basil
2 teaspoons cornstarch mixed with
  1 tablespoon water

Place the chicken in a large bowl with the lemongrass, chilies, garlic, ginger, and cilantro root. Mix together well.

Heat a wok over medium heat, add 1 teaspoon of the oil, and swirl to coat the surface of the wok. Add the cashews and cook for 1 minute or until lightly golden. Remove and drain on paper towels.

Heat the remaining oil in the wok, add the chicken in batches, and stir-fry over medium heat for 4–5 minutes or until browned. Return the chicken to the wok.

Stir in the lime juice, fish sauce, brown sugar, and basil, and cook for 30–60 seconds or until the basil just begins to wilt. Add the cornstarch mixture and stir until the mixture thickens slightly. Stir in the cashews and serve with steamed rice.

Serves 4

# Phad Thai

½ lb. flat dried rice stick noodles
1 small fresh red chili, chopped
2 cloves garlic, chopped
2 scallions, sliced
1 tablespoon tamarind purée,
  combined with 1 tablespoon water
1½ tablespoons sugar
2 tablespoons fish sauce
2 tablespoons lime juice
2 tablespoons vegetable oil
2 eggs, beaten
5 oz. pork tenderloin, thinly sliced
8 large shrimp, peeled, deveined, and
  tails intact
1 cup tofu puffs, julienned
1 cup bean sprouts
¼ cup chopped roasted peanuts
3 tablespoons fresh cilantro leaves
1 lime, cut into wedges

Soak the noodles in warm water for 10 minutes. Drain.

Pound the chili, garlic, and scallions in a mortar and pestle. Gradually blend in the tamarind mixture, sugar, fish sauce, and lime juice.

Heat a wok until very hot, add 1 tablespoon of the oil, and swirl to coat. Add the egg, swirl to coat, and cook for 1–2 minutes or until set and cooked. Remove and shred.

Heat the remaining oil, stir in the chili mixture, and stir-fry for 30 seconds. Add the sliced pork and stir-fry for 2 minutes or until tender. Add the shrimp and stir-fry for 1 minute more. Stir in the noodles, egg, tofu, and half the bean sprouts, and toss until heated through.

Serve immediately topped with the peanuts, cilantro, lime, and remaining bean sprouts.

Serves 4–6

## Japanese pork and noodle stir-fry

3/4 lb. pork tenderloin
1/3 cup soy sauce
1/4 cup mirin
2 teaspoons grated fresh ginger
2 cloves garlic, crushed
1 1/2 tablespoons light brown sugar
1 lb. Hokkien noodles
2 tablespoons peanut oil
1 onion, cut into thin wedges
1 red pepper, cut into thin strips
2 carrots, sliced finely and diagonally
4 scallions, sliced finely and
  diagonally
2 cups fresh shiitake mushrooms,
  sliced

Trim the pork of any excess fat or sinew and slice thinly. Combine the soy sauce, mirin, ginger, garlic, and brown sugar in a large nonmetallic bowl, add the pork, and coat. Cover with plastic wrap and refrigerate for 10 minutes.

Meanwhile, place the noodles in a bowl of hot water for 5 minutes to separate and soften.

Heat a large wok over high heat, add 1 tablespoon oil, and swirl to coat. Drain the pork, saving the marinade, and stir-fry in batches for 3 minutes or until browned. Remove and keep warm.

Reheat the wok over high heat, add the remaining oil, and swirl to coat. Add the onion, pepper, and carrots, and stir-fry for 2–3 minutes or until just tender, then add the scallions and shiitake mushrooms. Cook for another 2 minutes, then return the pork to the wok. Drain the noodles and add to the wok along with the marinade. Toss to combine and cook for another 1 minute or until heated through, then serve.

Serves 4

# Family beef stir-fry

2 tablespoons peanut oil
11-oz. fillet of beef, partially frozen
and thinly sliced
1 large onion, cut into thin wedges
1 red pepper, cut into thin strips
1 large carrot, sliced thinly and
diagonally
1 cup snow peas, sliced in half
diagonally
3/4 cup baby corn, sliced in half
diagonally
2 cups straw mushrooms, drained
2 tablespoons oyster sauce
1 clove garlic, crushed
1 teaspoon grated fresh ginger
2 tablespoons light soy sauce
2 tablespoons medium sherry
1 tablespoon honey
1 teaspoon sesame oil
2 teaspoons cornstarch

Heat a wok over high heat, add
1 tablespoon of the peanut oil, and
swirl around to coat the side of the
wok. Add the meat in batches and
cook for 2–3 minutes or until nicely
browned. Remove the meat from
the wok and keep warm.

Heat the remaining peanut oil in
the wok, add the onion, pepper,
and carrot, and cook, stirring, for
2–3 minutes or until the vegetables
are just tender. Add the snow peas,
corn, and straw mushrooms, cook
for another minute, then return all
the meat to the wok.

Combine the oyster sauce with
the garlic, ginger, soy sauce, sherry,
honey, sesame oil, and 1 tablespoon
water in a small bowl, then add
the mixture to the wok. Mix the
cornstarch with 1 tablespoon of
water, add to the wok, and cook for
1 minute or until the sauce thickens.
Season to taste with salt and freshly
ground black pepper. Serve
immediately with rice noodles or
thin egg noodles.

Serves 4

# Pork and brown bean noodles

3 tablespoons brown bean sauce
2 tablespoons hoisin sauce
3/4 cup chicken stock
1/2 teaspoon sugar
2 tablespoons peanut oil
3 cloves garlic, finely chopped
6 scallions, sliced, white and green
  parts separated
1 1/3 lbs. ground pork
1 lb. fresh Shanghai noodles
1 cucumber, halved lengthwise,
  seeded, and sliced diagonally
1 cup fresh cilantro leaves
1 cup bean sprouts
1 tablespoon lime juice

Combine the brown bean and hoisin sauces, stock, and sugar until smooth.

Heat the oil in a wok or large frying pan. Add the garlic and the white part of the scallions and cook for 10–20 seconds. Add the pork and cook over high heat for 2–3 minutes or until it has changed color. Add the bean mixture, reduce the heat, and simmer for 7–8 minutes.

Cook the noodles in a large saucepan of boiling water for 4–5 minutes or until tender. Drain and rinse, then divide among serving bowls. Toss together the cucumber, cilantro, bean sprouts, lime juice, and remaining scallions. Spoon the sauce over the noodles and top with the cucumber mixture.

Serves 4–6

## Stir-fried lamb with mint and chilies

1 tablespoon vegetable oil
1½-lb. lamb fillet, thinly sliced
  (see Note)
4 cloves garlic, finely chopped
2 small fresh red chilies, thinly sliced
⅓ cup oyster sauce
2½ tablespoons fish sauce
1½ teaspoons sugar
½ cup chopped fresh mint
¼ cup whole fresh mint leaves

Heat a wok over high heat, add the oil, and swirl to coat. Add the lamb and garlic in batches and stir-fry for 1–2 minutes or until the lamb is almost cooked. Return all the lamb to the wok. Stir in the chilies, oyster sauce, fish sauce, sugar, and the chopped mint leaves, and cook for another 1–2 minutes.

Remove from the heat, fold in the whole mint leaves, and serve immediately with rice.

Serves 4

Note: Make sure you slice the lamb across the grain—this will keep the meat from breaking up and shrinking too much when cooking.

# Ground chicken salad

1 tablespoon jasmine rice
2 teaspoons vegetable oil
3/4 lb. ground chicken
2 tablespoons fish sauce
1 lemongrass stalk, white part only,
  finely chopped
1/3 cup chicken stock
3 tablespoons lime juice
4 scallions, sliced finely and
  diagonally
4 red Asian shallots, sliced
1/2 cup finely chopped fresh cilantro
  leaves
1/2 cup shredded fresh mint
4 cups lettuce leaves, shredded
1/4 cup chopped roasted unsalted
  peanuts
1 small fresh red chili, sliced
lime wedges, to serve

Heat a frying pan. Add the rice and dry fry over low heat for 3 minutes or until lightly golden. Grind in a mortar and pestle to a fine powder.

Heat a wok over medium heat. Add the oil and ground chicken and cook for 4 minutes or until it changes color, breaking up any lumps. Add the fish sauce, lemongrass, and stock, and cook for another 10 minutes, then allow it to cool.

Add the lime juice, scallions, Asian shallots, cilantro, mint, and ground rice. Mix well.

Arrange the lettuce on a serving platter and top with the chicken mixture. Sprinkle with the nuts and chili and serve with lime wedges.

Serves 6

# Braised water spinach with tofu

1 lb. firm tofu (see Note)
1/4 cup vegetable oil
1 clove garlic, chopped
3/4 x 3/4-inch piece fresh ginger, chopped
1 1/2 lbs. water spinach, cut into 1 1/2-inch pieces
2 tablespoons kecap manis
2 tablespoons soy sauce
1 tablespoon roasted sesame seeds

Drain the tofu on paper towels and cut into 3/4-inch cubes. Heat a wok or large frying pan over high heat, add 2 tablespoons of the oil, and swirl to coat the surface of the wok. Add the tofu and cook, turning occasionally, for 5 minutes or until lightly browned. Drain on crumpled paper towels.

Heat the remaining oil in the wok, add the chopped garlic and ginger, and stir-fry for 1 minute. Stir in the water spinach, kecap manis, soy sauce, and 1 tablespoon water, toss well, then add the tofu and gently stir for 1 minute or until the water spinach has wilted. Sprinkle with the sesame seeds and serve immediately with rice.

Serves 4

Note: To reduce cooking time, you can use prefried tofu if available.
Variation: Any leafy Asian green spinach can replace the water spinach.

# Yakiudon

5 dried shiitake mushrooms
1 clove garlic, crushed
2 teaspoons grated fresh ginger
1/2 cup Japanese soy sauce
2 tablespoons rice wine vinegar
2 tablespoons sugar
1 tablespoon lemon juice
1 lb. fresh udon noodles
2 tablespoons vegetable oil
1 lb. skinless, boneless chicken
   thighs, thinly sliced
1 clove garlic, extra, finely chopped
1 small red pepper, thinly sliced
2 cups shredded cabbage
4 scallions, thinly sliced
1 tablespoon sesame oil
white pepper, to taste
2 tablespoons drained shredded
   pickled ginger

Place the mushrooms in a heatproof bowl and soak in boiling water for 10 minutes or until tender. Drain, saving 1/4 cup of the liquid. Discard the stems, squeeze the caps dry, and thinly slice.

Combine the crushed garlic, ginger, soy sauce, vinegar, sugar, lemon juice, and soaking liquid.

Place the noodles in a heatproof bowl, cover with boiling water, and leave for 2 minutes or until soft and tender. Drain.

Heat a wok over high heat, add half the oil, and swirl to coat. Add the chicken in batches and stir-fry for 5 minutes or until browned. Remove from the wok.

Add the remaining oil and swirl to coat. Add the extra chopped garlic, mushrooms, pepper, and cabbage, and stir-fry for 2–3 minutes or until softened. Add the noodles and stir-fry for another minute. Return the chicken to the wok and add the scallions, sesame oil, and soy sauce mixture, stirring until well combined and heated through. Season with white pepper and sprinkle with the pickled ginger.

Serves 4

# Sweet pork

1³/₄ lbs. pork spareribs
¹/₂ cup light brown sugar
4 red Asian shallots, sliced
1 tablespoon fish sauce
1 tablespoon kecap manis
¹/₂ teaspoon white pepper
¹/₃ cup loosely packed fresh
  cilantro leaves

Remove the bone and outer rind from the ribs. Cut into ¹/₂-inch slices.

Place the brown sugar in a wok with 2 tablespoons water and stir over low heat until the sugar dissolves. Increase to medium heat and boil, without stirring, for 5 minutes or until the sugar turns an even, golden brown. Add the pork and shallots and stir to coat. Add the fish sauce, kecap manis, pepper, and 1 cup warm water. Stir until any hard bits of sugar have melted.

Cover and cook for 10 minutes, stirring occasionally, then cook, uncovered and stirring often, for 20–30 minutes or until the sauce is sticky and the meat is cooked. Garnish with cilantro and serve with rice.

Serves 4–6

## Stir-fried scallops with sugar snap peas

2 tablespoons vegetable oil
2 large cloves garlic, crushed
3 teaspoons finely chopped
   fresh ginger
³/₄ lb. sugar snap peas
1 lb. scallops without roe,
   membrane removed
2 scallions, cut into ³/₄-inch
   pieces
2¹/₂ tablespoons oyster sauce
2 teaspoons soy sauce
¹/₂ teaspoon sesame oil
2 teaspoons sugar

Heat a wok over medium heat, add the oil, and swirl to coat the surface of the wok. Add the garlic and ginger and stir-fry for 30 seconds or until fragrant.

Add the peas to the wok and cook for 1 minute, then add the scallops and scallions and cook for 1 minute or until the scallions are wilted. Stir in the oyster and soy sauces, sesame oil, and sugar, and heat for 1 minute or until warmed through. Serve with rice.

Serves 4

## Chinese beef and broccoli stir-fry

¼ cup peanut oil
2 lbs. fresh rice noodle rolls, cut into
  ¾-inch strips, separated
1 lb. beef rump steak, trimmed and
  thinly sliced
1 onion, cut into wedges
4 cloves garlic, chopped
¾ lb. broccoli, cut into 1-inch pieces
1 tablespoon soy sauce
¼ cup kecap manis
1 small fresh red chili, chopped
½ cup beef stock

Heat a wok over medium heat, add
2 tablespoons of the peanut oil, and
swirl to coat the side of the wok.
Add the noodles and stir-fry gently
for 2 minutes. Remove from the wok.

Reheat the wok over high heat, add
the remaining oil, and swirl to coat.
Add the beef in batches and cook
for 3 minutes or until it is browned.
Remove from the wok. Add the
onion and stir-fry for 1–2 minutes,
then add the garlic and cook for
another 30 seconds.

Return all the beef to the wok and
add the broccoli, soy sauce, kecap
manis, chili, and beef stock, and
cook over medium heat for
2–3 minutes. Divide the rice
noodles among 4 large serving
bowls and top with the beef mixture.
Serve immediately.

Serves 4

Note: The noodles may break up
during cooking. This will not affect
the flavor of the dish.

# Singapore noodles

³/₄ lb. thin, fresh egg noodles
¹/₄ oz. dried Chinese mushrooms
2¹/₂ teaspoons sugar
1¹/₂ tablespoons soy sauce
2 tablespoons Chinese rice wine
1¹/₂ tablespoons curry powder
¹/₂ cup coconut milk
¹/₂ cup chicken stock
2 eggs
1 tablespoon sesame oil
3 tablespoons vegetable oil
2 cloves garlic, finely chopped
1 tablespoon finely chopped fresh
  ginger
2 small fresh red chilies, seeded
  and finely chopped
3 scallions, sliced
³/₄ lb. small shrimp, peeled, deveined,
  and halved
5 oz. Chinese roast pork, thinly sliced
1 cup frozen peas
fresh cilantro, to garnish

Cook the noodles in boiling salted water for 1 minute. Drain and rinse in cold water.

Soak the mushrooms in a bowl with ¹/₂ cup hot water for 10 minutes. Drain and save the liquid, then discard the hard stalks and finely slice the caps. Combine the soaking liquid with the sugar, soy sauce, rice wine, curry powder, coconut milk, and stock. Lightly beat the eggs and sesame oil together.

Heat a wok and add 2 tablespoons of the oil. Cook the garlic, ginger, chilies, and mushrooms for 30 seconds. Add the scallions, shrimp, roast pork, peas, and noodles. Stir in the mushroom liquid mixture. Add the egg mixture in a thin stream and toss until warmed through. Serve in deep bowls, garnished with fresh cilantro leaves.

Serves 4

## Pork and mushrooms with white pepper

½ oz. dried mushrooms
1 tablespoon peanut oil
¾ lb. pork fillet, thinly sliced
4 cloves garlic, thinly sliced
3 red Asian shallots, finely sliced
1 carrot, sliced finely and diagonally
6 scallions, cut into 1-inch pieces
2 tablespoons fish sauce
2 tablespoons oyster sauce
1 teaspoon ground white pepper

Soak the mushrooms in a bowl of boiling water for 20 minutes. Rinse, then cut into slices.

Heat a wok over medium heat, add the oil, and swirl to coat. Add the pork, garlic, and shallots, and stir-fry for 30 seconds. Add the carrot and scallions and stir-fry for 2–3 minutes or until the pork is no longer pink.

Add the mushrooms, fish and oyster sauces, and ground white pepper, and stir-fry for another minute. Serve hot with rice.

Serves 4

## Lamb with Hokkien noodles and sour sauce

1 lb. Hokkien noodles
2 tablespoons vegetable oil
3/4 lb. lamb fillet, thinly sliced against the grain
2/3 cup red Asian shallots, peeled and thinly sliced
3 cloves garlic, crushed
2 teaspoons finely chopped fresh ginger
1 small fresh red chili, seeded and finely chopped
1 1/2 tablespoons red curry paste
1 1/4 cups snow peas, trimmed and cut in half diagonally
1 small carrot, julienned
1/2 cup chicken stock
1 tablespoon light brown sugar
1 tablespoon lime juice
small whole basil leaves, to garnish

Cover the noodles with boiling water and soak for 1 minute. Drain and set aside.

Heat 1 tablespoon of the oil in a wok and swirl to coat. Stir-fry the lamb in batches over high heat for 2–3 minutes or until it just changes color. Remove to a side plate.

Add the remaining oil, then the shallots, garlic, ginger, and chili, and stir-fry for 1–2 minutes. Stir in the curry paste and cook for 1 minute. Add the snow peas, carrot, and the lamb, and combine. Cook over high heat, tossing often, for 1–2 minutes.

Add the stock, brown sugar, and lime juice, toss to combine, and cook for 2–3 minutes. Add the noodles and cook for 1 minute or until heated through. Divide among serving bowls and garnish with the basil.

Serves 4–6

## Noodles with beef

1 lb. unsliced, fresh rice noodles
2 tablespoons peanut oil
2 eggs, lightly beaten
1 lb. beef rump steak, thinly sliced
3 tablespoons kecap manis
1 1/2 tablespoons soy sauce
1 1/2 tablespoons fish sauce
3/4 lb. Chinese kale, cut into
   2-inch pieces
1/4 teaspoon white pepper
lemon wedges, to serve

Cut the noodles into 3/4-inch strips.
Gently separate the strips—run under
cold water if necessary.

Heat a wok over medium heat, add
1 tablespoon oil, and swirl to coat.
Add the egg, swirl to coat, and cook
for 1–2 minutes or until set. Remove
and slice.

Reheat the wok over high heat,
add the remaining oil, and swirl to
coat. Cook the beef in batches for
3 minutes or until brown. Remove.

Reduce the heat to medium, add the
noodles, and cook for 2 minutes.
Combine the kecap manis and soy
and fish sauces. Add to the wok with
the kale and white pepper, then
stir-fry for 2 minutes. Return the egg
and beef to the wok and cook for
3 minutes or until the kale has wilted
and the noodles are soft but not
breaking. Serve with the lemon.

Serves 4–6

Note: Rice noodles should not be
refrigerated, as they are very difficult
to separate when cold.

## Spicy eggplant stir-fry

1 tablespoon chili bean sauce
2 tablespoons soy sauce
1 tablespoon rice wine vinegar
1/2 teaspoon sugar
1/4 cup vegetable oil
1 lb. eggplant, cubed
1 yellow onion, cut into thin wedges
1 large fresh red chili, seeded,
  sliced diagonally
2 cloves garlic, crushed
1/2 cup fresh cilantro leaves

Place the chili bean sauce, soy sauce, rice wine vinegar, and sugar in a small bowl and whisk together well.

Heat a wok or frying pan over high heat, add 1 tablespoon of oil, and swirl to coat. Add half the eggplant and cook, stirring, for 3–4 minutes or until lightly browned all over. Drain on crumpled paper towels. Repeat with another tablespoon of oil and the remaining eggplant.

Reheat the wok over high heat, add the remaining oil, and swirl to coat. Add the onion, chili, and garlic, and cook over medium heat for 2 minutes. Return the eggplant to the wok, add the sauce, and cook, covered, for 5 minutes. Remove from the heat and stir in the cilantro leaves. Serve with rice.

Serves 4

Note: Chili bean sauce is used in many Szechuan-style dishes. If unavailable, replace it with garlic chili bean paste or sambal oelek, available from Asian food stores.

# Fried noodles with chicken, pork, and shrimp

2 lbs. fresh flat rice noodle sheets,
cut into 3/4-inch-thick slices
1/2 cup oil
2 cloves garlic, finely chopped
1 tablespoon grated fresh ginger
1/2 cup garlic chives, cut into
2-inch pieces
1/2 barbecued chicken, flesh cut into
1/2-inch slices
3/4 lb. barbecued pork fillet, cut into
1/2-inch slices
1 small fresh red chili, chopped
12 large cooked shrimp, peeled
and deveined
2 cups bean sprouts
2 cups spinach
2 eggs, beaten
2 teaspoons sugar
1/2 cup light soy sauce
2 tablespoons dark soy sauce
2 tablespoons fish sauce

Rinse the rice noodles under warm running water and carefully separate. Drain.

Heat a wok over high heat, add 1/4 cup of the oil, and swirl to coat. Add the garlic and ginger and cook, stirring, for 30 seconds. Be careful not to burn. Then add the chives and cook, stirring, for 10 seconds.

Add the barbecued chicken and pork, chili, and shrimp, and cook, stirring, for 2 minutes, then add the bean sprouts and spinach and cook, stirring, for 1 minute.

Make a well in the center of the mixture, add the egg, and scramble for 1 minute or until firm but not hard. Stir in the remaining oil, then add the rice noodles. Stir to combine. Add the combined sugar, light and dark soy sauce, and fish sauce, and stir-fry for 2–3 minutes or until heated through. Season with pepper.

Serves 4

## Shrimp and snow pea stir-fry

1 ½ tablespoons peanut oil
3 cloves garlic, thinly sliced
1 lemongrass stalk (white part only),
  finely chopped
1 ½ tablespoons thinly sliced fresh
  ginger
2 lbs. medium shrimp, peeled and
  deveined, with tails intact
2 cups snow peas, trimmed and cut
  into 3–4 strips lengthwise
6 scallions, cut into thin slices
  diagonally
1 ¼ cups snow pea sprouts
1 tablespoon Chinese rice wine or
  dry sherry
1 tablespoon oyster sauce
1 tablespoon soy sauce

Heat a wok to very hot, add the oil,
and swirl to coat the side. Add the
garlic, lemongrass, and ginger, and
stir-fry for 1–2 minutes or until
tragrant. Add the shrimp and cook
for 2–3 minutes or until they are
pink and cooked.

Add the snow peas, scallions,
sprouts, rice wine, oyster and soy
sauces, and toss until heated through
and the vegetables start to wilt.

Serves 4–6

# Mee grob

4 Chinese dried mushrooms
vegetable oil, for deep-frying
1/4 lb. dried rice vermicelli
2/3 cup fried tofu, cut into matchsticks
4 cloves garlic, crushed
1 onion, chopped
1 skinless, boneless chicken breast,
  thinly sliced
8 green beans, sliced diagonally
6 scallions, sliced thinly and
  diagonally
8 shrimp, peeled and deveined,
  tails intact
1/3 cup bean sprouts
fresh cilantro leaves, to garnish

*Sauce*
1 tablespoon soy sauce
3 tablespoons white vinegar
5 tablespoons sugar
3 tablespoons fish sauce
1 tablespoon sweet chili sauce

Soak the mushrooms in boiling water for 20 minutes. Drain the mushrooms, discard the stems, and slice thinly.

Fill a wok one-third full of oil and heat to 350°F or until a cube of bread browns in 15 seconds. Cook the vermicelli in small batches for 5 seconds or until puffed and crispy. Drain well.

Add the tofu to the wok in batches and deep-fry for 1 minute or until crisp. Drain. Carefully remove all but 2 tablespoons of the oil.

Reheat the wok until very hot. Add the garlic and onion and stir-fry for 1 minute. Add the chicken, beans, mushrooms, and half the scallions. Stir-fry for 2 minutes or until the chicken has almost cooked through. Add the shrimp and stir-fry for another 2 minutes or until they just turn pink.

Combine all the sauce ingredients and add to the wok. Stir-fry for 2 minutes or until the meat and shrimp are tender and the sauce is syrupy. Remove from the heat and stir in the vermicelli, tofu, and sprouts. Garnish with the cilantro and remaining scallion slices.

Serves 4–6

## Pork, asparagus, and baby corn stir-fry

1 clove garlic, chopped
1 teaspoon grated fresh ginger
2 tablespoons soy sauce
¼ teaspoon ground white pepper
1 tablespoon Chinese rice wine
1¼ lbs. pork fillet, thinly sliced
1 tablespoon peanut oil
1 teaspoon sesame oil
6 fresh shiitake mushrooms,
  thinly sliced
¾ cup baby corn
6 asparagus spears, cut diagonally
  into 1½-inch pieces
2 tablespoons oyster sauce

Place the garlic, ginger, soy sauce, pepper, and wine in a bowl and mix together well. Add all the pork and stir until it is well coated in the marinade.

Heat a wok over high heat, add half the oils, and swirl to coat the side of the wok. Add half the pork mixture and stir-fry for 2 minutes or until the pork changes color. Remove the pork from the wok. Repeat with the remaining oils and pork mixture.

Add the mushrooms, corn, and asparagus to the wok and stir-fry for 2 minutes. Return the pork and any juices to the wok and stir in the oyster sauce. Cook, stirring, for another 2 minutes or until it is evenly heated through. Divide among 4 plates and serve with rice.

Serves 4

## Chicken braised with ginger and star anise

1 teaspoon Szechuan peppercorns
2 tablespoons peanut oil
3/4 x 1 1/4-inch piece fresh ginger,
  julienned
2 cloves garlic, chopped
2 lbs. skinless, boneless chicken
  thighs, cut in half
1/3 cup Chinese rice wine
1 tablespoon honey
1/4 cup light soy sauce
1 star anise

Heat a wok over medium heat, add the peppercorns, and cook, stirring to prevent them from burning, for 2–4 minutes or until fragrant. Remove and lightly crush with the back of a knife.

Reheat the wok, add the oil, and swirl to coat. Add the ginger and garlic and cook over low heat for 1–2 minutes or until slightly golden. Add the chicken, increase the heat to medium, and cook for 3 minutes or until browned all over.

Add the peppercorns, wine, honey, soy sauce, and star anise to the wok, reduce the heat to low, and simmer, covered, for 20 minutes or until the chicken is tender. Divide among 4 plates and serve with steamed rice.

Serves 4

# Pork with plum sauce and choy sum

1 1/4 lbs. choy sum, cut into 2 1/2-inch
  pieces
1/2 cup peanut oil
1 large onion, sliced
3 cloves garlic, finely chopped
2 teaspoons finely chopped fresh
  ginger
1 lb. pork loin, thinly sliced
2 tablespoons cornstarch, seasoned
  with salt and pepper
1/4 cup plum sauce
1 1/2 tablespoons soy sauce
1 teaspoon sesame oil
2 tablespoons dry sherry or
  Chinese rice wine

Bring a large saucepan of lightly
salted water to a boil, add the choy
sum, and cook for 2–3 minutes or
until the stems are crisp but still
tender. Plunge into iced water
to chill completely, then drain.

Heat a wok over high heat, add
1 tablespoon oil, and swirl to coat.
Add the onion, garlic, and ginger,
and cook over medium heat for
3 minutes or until softened.
Remove from the wok.

Toss the pork in the seasoned
cornstarch to coat, shaking off any
excess. Reheat the wok over high
heat, add the remaining oil, and swirl
to coat. Add the pork in batches and
cook for 3 minutes or until golden
on both sides. Remove.

Drain the oil from the wok and return
the meat and any juices. Combine
the plum sauce, soy sauce, sesame
oil, and sherry, and add to the wok.
Cook over high heat for 2–3 minutes,
then add the choy sum and return
the onion mixture. Cook, stirring, for
another 2 minutes. Serve immediately
with rice.

Serves 4

# Chiang mai noodles

1/2 lb. fresh thin egg noodles
2 tablespoons oil
6 red Asian shallots, finely chopped
3 cloves garlic, crushed
1–2 small fresh red chilies, seeded
   and finely chopped
2–3 tablespoons red curry paste
3/4 lb. skinless, boneless chicken
   breasts, cut into thin strips
2 tablespoons fish sauce
1 tablespoon brown sugar
3 cups coconut milk
1 tablespoon lime juice
1 cup chicken stock
4 scallions, sliced, to garnish
1/3 cup fresh cilantro leaves,
   to garnish
fried red Asian shallot flakes,
   to garnish
store-bought fried noodles, to garnish
fresh red chili, finely diced, to garnish

Cook the noodles in a saucepan
of boiling water according to the
manufacturer's instructions. Drain,
cover, and set aside.

Heat a large wok over high heat,
add the oil, and swirl to coat. Add
the shallots, garlic, and chilies, and
stir-fry for 3 minutes. Stir in the curry
paste and stir-fry for 2 minutes. Add
the chicken and stir-fry for 3 minutes
or until it changes color.

Stir in the fish sauce, brown sugar,
coconut milk, lime juice, and stock.
Reduce the heat and simmer over
low heat for 5 minutes—do not boil.

To serve, divide the noodles among
4 deep serving bowls and spoon
in the chicken mixture. Garnish with
the scallions, cilantro, shallot flakes,
noodles, and diced chili.

Serves 4

# Vegetable and tofu puff stir-fry with barbecued pork

2 tablespoons peanut oil
1 tablespoon finely chopped fresh
  ginger
2 cloves garlic, chopped
2 cups snow peas, halved diagonally
  if large
1 carrot, sliced diagonally
1 small red pepper, thinly sliced
3/4 lb. bok choy, chopped
6 oz. fried tofu puffs, halved
3/4 lb. barbecued pork, thinly sliced
  (see Note)
2 tablespoons soy sauce
1/4 cup Chinese rice wine
2 tablespoons oyster sauce
1 fresh red chili, finely chopped
8 scallions, sliced diagonally

Heat a large wok or frying pan over high heat, add the oil, and swirl to coat. Add the ginger and garlic and cook for 30 seconds or until fragrant. Add the snow peas, carrots, red pepper, and bok choy, and stir-fry for 2–3 minutes or until just tender but still crisp. Add the tofu puffs and pork and toss to combine.

Add the soy sauce, rice wine, oyster sauce, and chili, and stir until heated through. Stir in the scallions and serve with jasmine rice.

Serves 4

Note: You can buy barbecued pork at Asian food stores or Chinese restaurants. It is precooked and is usually found in the takeout food section.

## Braised vegetables with cashews

1 tablespoon peanut oil
2 cloves garlic, crushed
2 teaspoons grated fresh ginger
3/4 lb. choy sum, cut into 4-inch
  pieces
3/4 cup baby corn, sliced in half
  diagonally
3/4 cup chicken or vegetable stock
3/4 cup canned, drained bamboo
  shoots
1 2/3 cups oyster mushrooms,
  sliced in half
2 teaspoons cornstarch
2 tablespoons oyster sauce
2 teaspoons sesame oil
1 cup bean sprouts
1/2 cup roasted unsalted cashews

Heat a wok over medium heat, add the oil, and swirl to coat. Add the garlic and ginger and stir-fry for 1 minute. Increase the heat to high, add the choy sum and baby corn, and stir-fry for another minute.

Add the chicken stock and cook for 3–4 minutes or until the choy sum stems are just tender. Add the bamboo shoots and mushrooms and cook for 1 minute.

Combine the cornstarch with 1 tablespoon water in a bowl. Stir into the vegetables with the oyster sauce. Cook for 1–2 minutes or until the sauce is slightly thickened. Stir in the sesame oil and sprouts and serve immediately on a bed of steamed rice sprinkled with the roasted cashews.

Serves 4

# Chili beef

¼ cup kecap manis
2½ teaspoons sambal oelek
2 cloves garlic, crushed
½ teaspoon ground cilantro
1 tablespoon light brown sugar
1 teaspoon sesame oil
¾-lb. beef fillet, partially frozen,
  thinly sliced
1 tablespoon peanut oil
2 tablespoons chopped roasted
  peanuts
3 tablespoons chopped fresh cilantro
  leaves

Combine the kecap manis, sambal oelek, crushed garlic, ground cilantro, brown sugar, sesame oil, and 2 tablespoons water in a large bowl. Add the beef slices and coat well. Cover with plastic wrap and refrigerate for 20 minutes.

Heat a wok over high heat, add the peanut oil, and swirl to coat. Add the meat in batches, cooking each batch for 2–3 minutes or until browned.

Arrange the beef on a serving platter, sprinkle with the chopped peanuts and fresh cilantro, and serve with steamed rice.

Serves 4

# Curries

# Musaman beef curry

1 tablespoon tamarind pulp
2 tablespoons vegetable oil
1½ lbs. lean stewing beef, cubed
2 cups coconut milk
4 cardamom pods, bruised
2 cups coconut cream
2–3 tablespoons prepared Musaman
   curry paste
2 tablespoons fish sauce
8 pickled onions, peeled
8 baby potatoes, peeled
2 tablespoons light brown sugar
½ cup unsalted peanuts, roasted
   and ground

Combine the tamarind pulp with ½ cup boiling water and set aside to cool. Mash the pulp with your fingertips to dissolve, then strain, saving the liquid.

Heat the oil in a wok. Add the beef in batches and cook over high heat for 5 minutes per batch or until browned. Reduce the heat, add the coconut milk and cardamom pods, and simmer for 1 hour or until the beef is tender. Remove the beef, then strain and save the cooking liquid.

Heat the coconut cream in the wok and stir in 2–3 tablespoons of the curry paste. Cook for 10 minutes or until it "cracks," or the oil separates from the cream. Add the fish sauce, onions, potatoes, beef mixture, brown sugar, peanuts, tamarind water, and the straining liquid. Simmer for 25–30 minutes.

Serves 4

## Rogan josh

2-lb. boneless leg of lamb
1 tablespoon ghee or butter
2 onions, chopped
½ cup plain yogurt
1 teaspoon chili powder
1 tablespoon ground cilantro
2 teaspoons ground cumin
1 teaspoon ground cardamom
½ teaspoon ground cloves
1 teaspoon ground turmeric
3 cloves garlic, crushed
1 tablespoon grated fresh ginger
14-oz. can diced tomatoes
¼ cup slivered almonds
1 teaspoon garam masala
chopped fresh cilantro leaves,
  to garnish

Trim the lamb of any excess fat and sinew and cut it into 1-inch cubes.

Heat the ghee in a large saucepan, add the onions, and cook, stirring, for 5 minutes or until soft. Stir in the yogurt, chili powder, cilantro, cumin, cardamom, cloves, turmeric, garlic, and ginger. Add the tomatoes and 1 teaspoon salt and simmer for 5 minutes.

Add the lamb and stir until coated. Cover and cook over low heat, stirring occasionally, for 1–1½ hours or until the lamb is tender. Remove the lid and simmer until the liquid thickens.

Meanwhile, roast the almonds in a dry frying pan over medium heat for 3–4 minutes, shaking the pan gently, until the nuts are golden brown. Remove from the pan at once to keep them from burning.

Add the garam masala to the curry and mix through well. Sprinkle the slivered almonds and cilantro leaves over the top and serve.

Serves 4–6

# Butter chicken

2 tablespoons peanut oil
2 lbs. skinless, boneless chicken
  thighs, quartered
1/4 cup butter or ghee
2 teaspoons garam masala
2 teaspoons sweet paprika
2 teaspoons ground cilantro
1 tablespoon finely chopped fresh
  ginger
1/4 teaspoon chili powder
1 cinnamon stick
6 cardamom pods, bruised
3/4 lb. puréed tomatoes
1 tablespoon sugar
1/4 cup plain yogurt
1/2 cup whipping cream
1 tablespoon lemon juice

Heat a wok until very hot, add
1 tablespoon oil, and swirl to coat.
Add half the chicken and stir-fry for
4 minutes or until browned. Remove.
Add extra oil, as needed, and cook
the remaining chicken. Remove.

Reduce the heat, add the butter
to the wok, and melt. Add the garam
masala, sweet paprika, cilantro,
ginger, chili powder, cinnamon stick,
and cardamom pods, and stir-fry for
1 minute or until fragrant. Return the
chicken to the wok and mix to coat
in the spices.

Add the tomatoes and sugar and
simmer, stirring, for 15 minutes
or until the chicken is tender
and the sauce has thickened.

Add the yogurt, cream, and juice,
and simmer for 5 minutes or until
the sauce has thickened slightly.
Serve with rice and flatbread.

Serves 4–6

# Yellow curry with vegetables

*Yellow curry paste*
8 small dried red chilies
1 teaspoon black peppercorns
2 teaspoons cilantro seeds
2 teaspoons cumin seeds
1 teaspoon ground turmeric
1½ tablespoons chopped fresh
  galangal
5 cloves garlic, chopped
1 teaspoon grated fresh ginger
5 red Asian shallots, chopped
2 lemongrass stalks, white part only,
  chopped
1 teaspoon shrimp paste
1 teaspoon finely chopped lime zest

2 tablespoons peanut oil
2 cups coconut cream
½ cup vegetable stock
1½ cups snake beans, cut into
  1-inch pieces
¾ cup fresh baby corn
1 slender eggplant, cut into ½-inch
  slices
¾ cup small cauliflower florets
2 small zucchini, cut into ½-inch
  slices
1 small red pepper, cut into
  ½-inch slices
1½ tablespoons fish sauce
1 teaspoon light brown sugar
1 small fresh red chili, chopped,
  to garnish
fresh cilantro leaves, to garnish

To make the curry paste, soak
the chilies in boiling water for
15 minutes. Drain and chop. Heat
a frying pan, add the peppercorns,
cilantro seeds, cumin seeds, and
turmeric, and dry fry over medium
heat for 3 minutes. Transfer to a
mortar and pestle or food processor
and grind to a fine powder.

Place the ground spices, chilies,
galangal, garlic, ginger, shallots,
lemongrass, and shrimp paste in
a mortar and pestle and pound
until smooth. Stir in the lime zest.

Heat a wok over medium heat,
add the oil, and swirl to coat. Add
2 tablespoons of the curry paste
and cook for 1 minute. Add 1 cup
of coconut cream and cook over
medium heat for 10 minutes or
until the mixture is thick and the
oil separates.

Add the stock, vegetables, and
remaining coconut cream, and cook
for 5 minutes or until the vegetables
are tender, but still crisp. Stir in the
fish sauce and sugar and garnish
with the chopped chili and cilantro.

Serves 4

## Madras beef curry

1 tablespoon butter or ghee
1 onion, chopped
3–4 tablespoons Madras curry paste
2 lbs. boneless beef skirt or chuck
  steak, trimmed and cut into
  1-inch cubes
¼ cup tomato paste
1 cup beef stock

Heat the butter in a large frying pan, add the onion, and cook over medium heat for 10 minutes or until browned. Add the curry paste and stir for 1 minute or until fragrant.

Add the meat and cook, stirring until coated with the curry paste. Stir in the tomato paste and beef stock. Reduce the heat and simmer, covered, for 1 hour, 15 minutes, and then uncovered for 15 minutes or until the meat is tender.

Serves 4

# Thai jungle curry shrimp

*Curry paste*
10–12 dried red chilies
4 red Asian shallots, chopped
4 cloves garlic, sliced
1 lemongrass stalk, white part only,
  sliced
1 tablespoon finely chopped fresh
  galangal
2 small cilantro roots, chopped
1 tablespoon finely chopped fresh
  ginger
1 tablespoon shrimp paste,
  dry roasted
1/4 cup vegetable oil

1 tablespoon oil
1 clove garlic, crushed
1/4 cup ground candlenuts or
  macadamias
1 tablespoon fish sauce
1 1/4 cups fish stock
1 tablespoon whiskey
1 1/4 lbs. shrimp, peeled, deveined,
  with tails intact
1 small carrot, slivered
1 2/3 cups snake beans, cut into
  3/4-inch pieces
1/4 cup bamboo shoots
3 kaffir lime leaves, crushed
fresh Thai basil leaves, to garnish

To make the curry paste, soak
the chilies in 1 cup boiling water for
10 minutes, then drain and place in
a food processor with the remaining
curry paste ingredients. Season with
salt and white pepper and process
to a smooth paste.

Heat a wok over medium heat, add
the oil, and stir to coat the side. Add
3 tablespoons of the curry paste
and the garlic and cook, stirring
constantly, for 5 minutes or until
fragrant. Stir in the candlenuts,
fish sauce, stock, whiskey, shrimp,
vegetables, and lime leaves, and
bring to a boil. Reduce the heat
and simmer for 5 minutes or until
the shrimp and vegetables are
cooked through. Garnish with the
Thai basil leaves and black pepper.

Serves 6

# Goan pork curry

2 teaspoons cumin seeds
2 teaspoons black mustard seeds
1 teaspoon cardamom seeds
1 teaspoon ground turmeric
1 teaspoon ground cinnamon
1/2 teaspoon black peppercorns
6 whole cloves
5 small dried red chilies
1/3 cup white vinegar
1 tablespoon light brown sugar
1/3 cup oil
1 large onion, chopped
6–8 cloves garlic, crushed
1 tablespoon finely grated fresh
    ginger
3-lb. boneless pork leg, cut into
    1-inch cubes

Dry fry the spices and chilies in a large frying pan for 2 minutes or until fragrant. Place in a spice grinder or food processor and grind until finely ground. Transfer to a bowl and stir in the vinegar, sugar, and 1 teaspoon salt to form a paste.

Heat half the oil in a large saucepan. Add the chopped onion and cook for 5 minutes or until lightly golden. Place the onion in a food processor with 2 tablespoons cold water and process until smooth. Stir into the spice paste.

Place the garlic and ginger in a small bowl, mix together well, and stir in 2 tablespoons water.

Heat the remaining oil in the saucepan over high heat. Add the cubed pork and cook in 3–4 batches for 8 minutes or until well browned. Return all the meat to the saucepan and stir in the garlic and ginger mixture. Add the onion mixture and 1 cup hot water. Simmer, covered, for 1 hour or until the pork is tender. Uncover, bring to a boil, and cook, stirring frequently, for 10 minutes or until the sauce reduces and thickens slightly. Serve with rice and flatbread.

Serves 6

## Quick duck curry

2-lb. Peking duck (see Note)
1 tablespoon vegetable oil
1 red onion, finely chopped
2 cloves garlic, crushed
1 fresh red chili, seeded and chopped
1 tablespoon red curry paste
1 tablespoon smooth peanut butter
1 2/3 cups coconut milk
1 1/4 cups chicken stock
1 tablespoon lime juice
1 tablespoon fish sauce
2 tablespoons chopped fresh cilantro
   leaves

Remove the skin and bones from the Peking duck and cut the meat into bite-size pieces.

Heat the oil in a saucepan over medium heat, add the onion, and cook for 5 minutes. Add the garlic and chili and cook for 2 minutes. Stir in the curry paste and cook for 1–2 minutes or until fragrant, then stir in the peanut butter.

Gradually whisk in the coconut milk and cook for 2 minutes or until thoroughly combined. Add the stock, bring to a boil, then reduce the heat and simmer for 10 minutes. Add the duck and simmer for 10 minutes. Stir in the lime juice and fish sauce. Sprinkle the cilantro over the top and serve with rice or noodles.

Serves 4

Note: Peking duck is available from Asian food stores. Leave the skin on the duck if preferred.

# Panang beef

*Paste*
8–10 large dried red chilies
6 red Asian shallots, chopped
6 cloves garlic, chopped
1 teaspoon ground cilantro
1 tablespoon ground cumin
1 teaspoon white pepper
2 lemongrass stalks, white part only,
  lightly smashed and sliced
1 tablespoon chopped fresh galangal
6 fresh cilantro roots
2 teaspoons shrimp paste
2 tablespoons roasted peanuts

1 tablespoon peanut oil
1²/₃ cups coconut cream
2 lbs. round or blade steak, cut into
  ½-inch slices
1²/₃ cups coconut milk
⅓ cup crunchy peanut butter
4 fresh kaffir lime leaves
3 tablespoons lime juice
2½ tablespoons fish sauce
3–4 tablespoons light brown sugar
1 tablespoon chopped roasted
  peanuts, to garnish
fresh Thai basil, to garnish

To make the paste, soak the chilies in a large bowl of boiling water for 15 minutes or until soft. Remove the seeds and chop. Place in a food processor with the shallots, garlic, ground cilantro, ground cumin, white pepper, lemongrass, galangal, cilantro roots, shrimp paste, and peanuts, and process until smooth. Add a little water if the paste is too thick.

Place the peanut oil and the thick coconut cream from the top of the can (set aside the rest) in a saucepan and cook over medium heat for 10 minutes or until the oil separates. Add 6–8 tablespoons of the paste and cook, stirring, for 5–8 minutes or until fragrant.

Add the beef, coconut milk, peanut butter, lime leaves, and the remaining coconut cream. Cook for 8 minutes or until the beef just starts to change color. Reduce the heat and simmer for 1 hour or until the beef is tender. Stir in the lime juice, fish sauce, and sugar. Serve garnished with the peanuts and Thai basil.

Serves 4–6

## Malaysian Nonya chicken curry

*Curry paste*
2 red onions, chopped
4 small fresh red chilies, seeded
  and sliced
4 cloves garlic, sliced
2 lemongrass stalks, white part
  only, sliced
3/4 x 1 1/4-inch piece galangal, sliced
8 kaffir lime leaves, roughly chopped
1 teaspoon ground turmeric
1/2 teaspoon shrimp paste,
  dry roasted

2 tablespoons vegetable oil
1 1/2 lbs. skinless, boneless chicken
  thighs, cut into bite-size pieces
1 2/3 cups coconut milk
3 tablespoons tamarind purée
1 tablespoon fish sauce
3 kaffir lime leaves, shredded

To make the curry paste, place all of the ingredients in a food processor or blender and process to a thick paste.

Heat a wok or large saucepan over high heat, add the oil, and swirl to coat the side. Add the curry paste and cook, stirring occasionally, over low heat for 8–10 minutes or until fragrant. Add the chicken and stir-fry with the paste for 2–3 minutes.

Add the coconut milk, tamarind purée, and fish sauce to the wok and simmer, stirring occasionally, for 15–20 minutes or until the chicken is tender. Garnish with the lime leaves. Serve with rice and steamed bok choy.

Serves 4

# Lamb kofta

2 lbs. ground lamb
1 onion, finely chopped
2 small fresh green chilies, finely
  chopped
3 teaspoons grated fresh ginger
3 cloves garlic, crushed
1/3 cup fresh breadcrumbs
1 egg, lightly beaten
1 teaspoon ground cardamom
2 tablespoons ghee or butter

*Sauce*
1 tablespoon ghee or butter
1 onion, sliced
1 fresh green chili, finely chopped
3 teaspoons grated fresh ginger
2 cloves garlic, crushed
1 teaspoon ground turmeric
3 teaspoons ground cilantro
2 teaspoons ground cumin
1 teaspoon chili powder
2 tablespoons white vinegar
3/4 cup plain yogurt
1 1/4 cups coconut milk

Line a baking tray with waxed paper or plastic wrap. Place the ground lamb in a large bowl with the onion, chilies, ginger, garlic, breadcrumbs, egg, and cardamom. Season and mix together. Roll level tablespoons of the mixture into balls and place on the baking tray.

Heat the ghee in a large frying pan, add the meatballs in batches, and cook over medium heat for 10 minutes or until browned all over.

To make the sauce, heat the ghee in the same pan, add the onion, chili, ginger, garlic, and turmeric, and cook, stirring, over low heat for 8 minutes or until the onion is soft. Add the cilantro, cumin, chili powder, vinegar, meatballs, and 1 1/3 cups water, and stir gently. Simmer, covered, for 30 minutes. Stir in the combined yogurt and coconut milk and simmer, partially covered, for another 10 minutes. Serve with rice.

Serves 4–6

# Yellow fish curry

½ cup vegetable stock
1 tablespoon store-bought yellow
  curry paste (see Note)
1 tablespoon tamarind purée
1 tablespoon light brown sugar
1½ tablespoons fish sauce
1¼ cups green beans, trimmed and
  cut into 1½-inch pieces
1 cup sliced, canned bamboo shoots,
  rinsed and drained
1⅔ cups coconut cream
¾ lb. perch fillet, skin removed,
  cubed
1 tablespoon lime juice
lime wedges, to serve
fresh cilantro leaves, to garnish

Place the vegetable stock in a large saucepan and bring to a boil. Add the curry paste and cook, stirring, for 3–4 minutes or until fragrant. Stir in the combined tamarind purée, brown sugar, and 1 tablespoon of the fish sauce. Add the beans and bamboo shoots and cook over medium heat for 3–5 minutes or until the beans are almost tender.

Add the coconut cream and bring to a boil, then reduce the heat, add the fish, and simmer for 3–5 minutes or until the fish is just cooked. Stir in the lime juice and remaining fish sauce. Garnish with the lime wedges and cilantro leaves. Serve with rice.

Serves 4

Note: Yellow curry paste can be bought at some supermarkets and Asian food stores.

# Chickpea curry

1 cup dried chickpeas
2 tablespoons vegetable oil
2 onions, finely chopped
2 large ripe tomatoes, chopped
1/2 teaspoon ground cilantro
1 teaspoon ground cumin
1 teaspoon chili powder
1/4 teaspoon ground turmeric
1 tablespoon channa (chole) masala
   (see Note)
1 tablespoon ghee or butter
1 small onion, sliced
fresh mint and cilantro leaves,
   to garnish

Place the chickpeas in a bowl, cover with water, and allow to soak overnight. Drain, rinse, and place in a large saucepan. Cover with plenty of water and bring to a boil, then reduce the heat and simmer for 40 minutes or until soft. Drain.

Heat the oil in a large saucepan, add the onions, and cook over medium heat for 15 minutes or until golden brown. Add the tomatoes, cilantro, cumin, chili powder, turmeric, channa (chole) masala, and 2 cups water, and cook for 10 minutes or until the tomatoes are soft. Add the chickpeas, season well with salt, and cook for 8 minutes or until the sauce thickens. Transfer to a serving dish. Place the ghee or butter on top and allow to melt before serving. Garnish with the sliced onion and the mint and cilantro leaves.

Serves 6

Note: Channa (chole) masala is a spice blend specifically used in this dish. It is available at Indian grocery stores. Garam masala can be used as a substitute if it is unavailable, but this will alter the final flavor.

# Green chicken curry

*Curry paste*
1/2 teaspoon cumin seeds, roasted
1 teaspoon cilantro seeds, toasted
1/4 teaspoon white peppercorns
5 fresh cilantro roots
3 tablespoons chopped fresh
  galangal
10 fresh long green chilies, chopped
1 lemongrass stalk, chopped
6 red Asian shallots
3 cloves garlic, peeled
1 tablespoon shrimp paste
1 teaspoon grated kaffir lime or
  lime zest
2 tablespoons peanut oil

1 cup thick coconut cream
1 lb. skinless, boneless chicken
  thighs, thinly sliced
2 cups coconut milk
1 cup snake beans, cut into
  1-inch pieces
2 1/2 cups small broccoli florets
1 tablespoon light brown sugar
2–3 tablespoons fish sauce
5 tablespoons fresh cilantro leaves

To make the curry paste, place the cumin seeds, cilantro seeds, and peppercorns in a spice grinder or mortar and pestle and grind into a fine powder. Place the powder in a food processor with 1/4 teaspoon salt and the remaining paste ingredients and process until smooth.

Place the coconut cream in a wok, bring to a boil over high heat, and cook for 10 minutes or until the oil separates, giving a thicker curry.

Reduce the heat to medium. Stir in half the curry paste and cook for 2–3 minutes or until fragrant. Add the chicken pieces and cook for 3–4 minutes or until almost cooked. Stir in the coconut milk, beans, and broccoli. Bring to a boil, then reduce the heat and simmer for 4–5 minutes or until the chicken and vegetables are cooked. Stir in the brown sugar, fish sauce, and cilantro. Serve with steamed rice and garnish with extra cilantro leaves, if desired.

Serves 4

Note: Store any leftover paste in an airtight container in the freezer for up to three months.

# Fish ball curry

1 large onion, chopped
1 teaspoon sambal oelek
1 tablespoon finely chopped fresh
  ginger
1 lemongrass stalk, white part only,
  finely chopped
3 tablespoons fresh chopped
  cilantro roots
½ teaspoon ground cardamom
1 tablespoon tomato paste
1 tablespoon oil
1 tablespoon fish sauce
2 cups coconut milk
1½ lbs. fish balls (thawed, if frozen)
3 tablespoons chopped fresh
  coriander
fresh cilantro, extra, to garnish

Place the onion, sambal oelek, ginger, lemongrass, cilantro, cardamom, and tomato paste in a food processor and process to a smooth paste.

Heat the oil in a large saucepan. Add the spice paste and cook, stirring, over medium heat for 4 minutes or until fragrant.

Stir in the fish sauce, coconut milk, and 2 cups water. Bring to a boil, then reduce the heat and simmer for 15 minutes or until the sauce has reduced and thickened slightly.

Add the fish balls and cook for 2 minutes. Do not overcook or the fish balls will be tough and rubbery. Stir in the cilantro and garnish with extra cilantro. Serve with rice.

Serves 6

# Indian-style butter shrimp

2 lbs. large shrimp
1/2 cup butter
2 large cloves garlic, crushed
1 teaspoon ground cumin
1 teaspoon paprika
1 1/2 teaspoons garam masala
2 tablespoons good-quality,
  store-bought tandoori paste
2 tablespoons tomato paste
1 1/4 cups whipping cream
1 teaspoon sugar
1/3 cup plain yogurt
2 tablespoons chopped fresh
  cilantro leaves
1 tablespoon sliced almonds,
  roasted
lemon wedges, to serve

Peel and devein the shrimp, leaving the tails intact. Melt the butter in a large saucepan over medium heat, then add the garlic, cumin, paprika, and 1 teaspoon of the garam masala, and cook for 1 minute or until fragrant. Add the tandoori paste and tomato paste and cook for another 2 minutes. Stir in the cream and sugar, then reduce the heat and simmer for 10 minutes or until the sauce thickens slightly.

Add the shrimp to the saucepan and cook for 8–10 minutes or until they are pink and cooked through. Remove the saucepan from the heat and stir in the yogurt, the remaining garam masala, and half the cilantro. Season.

Garnish with the sliced almonds and remaining cilantro and serve with steamed rice and lemon wedges.

Serves 4

Note: This dish is very rich, so we recommend that you serve it with steamed vegetables or a fresh salad.

# Thai beef and squash curry

2 tablespoons vegetable oil
1½ lbs. blade steak, thinly sliced
  (see Note)
4 tablespoons Musaman curry paste
2 cloves garlic, finely chopped
1 onion, sliced lengthwise
6 curry leaves, torn
3 cups coconut milk
3 cups butternut squash,
  roughly diced
2 tablespoons chopped unsalted
  peanuts
1 tablespoon light brown sugar
2 tablespoons tamarind purée
2 tablespoons fish sauce
curry leaves, to garnish

Heat a wok or frying pan over high heat. Add the oil and swirl to coat the side. Add the meat in batches and cook for 5 minutes or until browned. Remove the meat from the wok.

Add the curry paste, garlic, onion, and curry leaves to the wok and stir to coat. Return the meat to the wok and cook, stirring, over medium heat for 2 minutes.

Add the coconut milk to the wok, then reduce the heat and simmer for 45 minutes. Add the diced squash and simmer for 25–30 minutes or until the meat and the vegetables are tender and the sauce has thickened.

Stir in the peanuts, brown sugar, tamarind purée, and fish sauce, and simmer for 1 minute. Garnish with curry leaves. Serve with pickled vegetables and rice.

Serves 6

Note: Cut the meat into ¾ x 2 x 2-inch pieces, then cut across the grain at a 45-degree angle into ¼-inch-thick slices.

# Lamb korma

2 tablespoons blanched almonds
2 teaspoons grated fresh ginger
4 cloves garlic, crushed
½ teaspoon ground cinnamon
½ teaspoon ground cardamom
¼ teaspoon ground cloves
½ teaspoon chili powder
½ teaspoon ground mace
1½ teaspoons paprika
1 teaspoon ground coriander
⅓ cup ghee or butter
2 onions, thinly sliced
2-lb. boneless leg of lamb, cubed
¼ teaspoon saffron threads, soaked
   in 1 tablespoon warm water
1 cup plain yogurt
½ cup sour cream
fresh cilantro sprigs, to garnish

Place the almonds, ginger, and garlic in a blender with ¼ cup water. Blend until smooth. Add the ground spices and blend for 10 seconds or until combined.

Heat the ghee in a casserole dish, add the onions, and cook over medium heat for 10–15 minutes or until caramelized. Add the spice paste and cook, stirring to prevent sticking, for 5 minutes or until fragrant.

Add the meat and toss to coat in the spices. Cook, stirring, for 5 minutes or until browned.

Add the saffron and soaking liquid, half the yogurt, and half the sour cream. Season with salt and bring to a boil, then reduce the heat and simmer, covered, for 2 hours or until the meat is tender. Stir frequently to keep from sticking, as the curry is quite dry when cooked. Skim any fat from the surface. Stir in the remaining yogurt and sour cream and garnish with the cilantro. Serve with rice.

Serves 4–6

# Chicken curry with apricots

18 dried apricots
1 tablespoon ghee or butter
2 3-lb. chickens, cut up
3 onions, finely sliced
1 teaspoon grated fresh ginger
3 cloves garlic, crushed
3 large fresh green chilies, seeded
  and finely chopped
1 teaspoon cumin seeds
1 teaspoon chili powder
½ teaspoon ground turmeric
4 cardamom pods, lightly smashed
4 large tomatoes, peeled and cut
  into eighths

Soak the dried apricots in 1 cup hot water for 1 hour.

Melt the ghee in a large saucepan, add the chicken pieces in batches, and cook over high heat for 5–6 minutes or until browned. Remove from the saucepan. Add the onions and cook, stirring often, for 10 minutes or until the onions are softened and golden brown.

Add the ginger, garlic, and chopped green chilies, and cook, stirring, for 2 minutes. Stir in the cumin seeds, chili powder, and ground turmeric, and cook for another minute.

Return the chicken to the saucepan, add the cardamoms, tomatoes, and apricots, along with any remaining liquid, and mix well. Simmer, covered, for 35 minutes or until the chicken is tender.

Remove the chicken, cover, and keep warm. Bring the liquid to a boil and boil rapidly, uncovered, for 5 minutes or until it has thickened slightly. Spoon the liquid over the chicken and serve with steamed rice mixed with raisins, grated carrot, and toasted sliced almonds.

Serves 6–8

# Light red seafood curry

*Chu chee paste*
10 large dried red chilies
1 tablespoon shrimp paste
1 tablespoon white peppercorns
1 teaspoon coriander seeds
2 teaspoons finely grated
  kaffir lime zest
10 fresh kaffir lime leaves, finely
  shredded
1 tablespoon chopped fresh cilantro
  stem
1 lemongrass stalk, white part only,
  finely chopped
3 tablespoons chopped fresh galangal
6 cloves garlic, chopped
10 red Asian shallots, chopped

2¼ cups canned coconut milk
1 lb. large shrimp, peeled, deveined,
  with tails intact
1 lb. scallops, without roe
2–3 tablespoons fish sauce
2–3 tablespoons light brown sugar
8 fresh kaffir lime leaves, finely
  shredded
2 small fresh red chilies, thinly sliced,
  (optional)
1 cup fresh Thai basil

Soak the chilies in hot water for
15 minutes. Drain, remove the
seeds, and chop. Preheat the oven
to 350°F. Put the shrimp paste,
peppercorns, and coriander seeds on
a baking tray lined with aluminum foil
and bake for 5 minutes.

Blend the baked spices in a food
processor with the remaining paste
ingredients until smooth.

Remove 1 cup thick coconut cream
from the top of the cans (save the
rest) and place in a wok. Heat until
just boiling, then stir in 3 tablespoons
of the curry paste. Reduce the heat.
Simmer for 10 minutes or until the
mixture is fragrant and the oil begins
to separate.

Stir in the seafood and remaining
coconut cream and cook for
5 minutes. Add the fish sauce,
sugar, lime leaves, and chilies, and
cook for 1 minute. Stir in half the
basil and use the rest to garnish.

Serves 4

# Paneer and pea curry

*Paneer*
8 cups whole milk
1/3 cup lemon juice
vegetable oil, for deep-frying

*Curry paste*
2 large onions
3 cloves garlic
1 teaspoon grated fresh ginger
1 teaspoon cumin seeds
3 dried red chilies
1 teaspoon cardamom seeds
4 cloves
1 teaspoon fennel seeds
2 pieces cassia bark

1 lb. frozen peas
2 tablespoons oil
3/4 lb. puréed tomatoes
1 tablespoon garam masala
1 teaspoon ground coriander
1/4 teaspoon ground turmeric
1 tablespoon cream
fresh cilantro leaves, to garnish

Bring the milk to a boil in a large saucepan, stir in the lemon juice, and turn off the heat. Stir the mixture for a few seconds as it curdles. Place in a colander and leave for 30 minutes to allow the whey to drain off. Place the paneer curds on a clean, flat surface, cover with a plate, weigh down, and leave for at least 4 hours.

To make the curry paste, place all the ingredients in a spice grinder and grind to a smooth paste.

Cut the solid paneer into 3/4-inch cubes. Fill a deep, heavy-bottomed saucepan one-third full of oil and heat to 350°F or until a cube of bread browns in 15 seconds. Cook the paneer in batches for 2 minutes per batch or until golden. Drain on paper towels. Bring a saucepan of water to a boil, add the peas, and cook for 3 minutes or until tender. Drain.

Heat the oil in a large saucepan, add the curry paste, and cook over medium heat for 4 minutes or until fragrant. Add the puréed tomatoes, spices, cream, and 1/2 cup water. Season with salt and simmer for 5 minutes. Add the paneer and peas and cook for 3 minutes. Garnish with cilantro leaves and serve hot.

Serves 6

# Beef rendang

2 lbs. beef round or chuck, cut into
 ½-inch-thick strips
2 onions, chopped
1 tablespoon chopped fresh ginger
3 cloves garlic, finely chopped
1 teaspoon ground turmeric
2 teaspoons ground coriander
2½ tablespoons sambal oelek
½ cup vegetable oil
1⅔ cups coconut cream
6 fresh curry leaves
1 lemongrass stalk, lightly smashed
½ cup tamarind purée
4 kaffir lime leaves
1 teaspoon light brown sugar
1 kaffir lime leaf, extra, shredded,
 to garnish

Season the beef with salt and white pepper. Place the onions, ginger, garlic, turmeric, coriander, and sambal oelek in a blender and blend until smooth. Add a little water if necessary.

Heat the oil in a large saucepan, add the spice paste, and cook over medium heat for 5 minutes or until fragrant. Add the beef, stir to coat in the spices, and cook for 1–2 minutes. Add the coconut cream, curry leaves, lemongrass, tamarind purée, lime leaves, and 2 cups water. Reduce the heat and simmer over low heat for 2½ hours or until the meat is tender and the sauce has thickened. Add a little water, if necessary, to keep the sauce from sticking. Stir in the sugar. Garnish with the shredded kaffir lime leaf and serve with rice.

Serves 4

# Malaysian hot and sour pineapple curry

1 half-ripe pineapple, cored and
  cut into chunks
1/2 teaspoon ground turmeric
1 star anise
7 cloves
1 cinnamon stick, broken into
  small pieces
7 cardamom pods, lightly smashed
1 tablespoon vegetable oil
1 onion, finely chopped
1 teaspoon grated fresh ginger
1 clove garlic
5 fresh red chilies, chopped
1 tablespoon sugar
1/4 cup coconut cream

Place the pineapple in a saucepan, cover with water, and add the ground turmeric. Wrap the star anise, cloves, cinnamon, and cardamom pods in a square of cheesecloth and tie securely with string. Add to the saucepan and cook over medium heat for 10 minutes. Squeeze the bag to extract any flavor, then discard.

Heat the oil in a frying pan, add the onion, ginger, garlic, and chilies, and cook, stirring, for 1–2 minutes or until fragrant. Add the pineapple and the cooking liquid, sugar, and salt to taste. Cook for 2 minutes, then stir in the coconut cream. Cook, stirring, over low heat for 3–5 minutes or until the sauce thickens. Serve hot or cold.

Serves 6

Note: This dish is very popular with children due to its color and sweetness, but you might want to cut back on the chilies! If the pineapple is too ripe, this dish will turn to mush, so it is important to make sure you use a half-ripe pineapple, which will keep its shape during cooking.

# Sri Lankan chicken curry with cashews

*Curry powder*
3 tablespoons coriander seeds
1 1/2 tablespoons cumin seeds
1 teaspoon fennel seeds
1/4 teaspoon fenugreek seeds
1-inch cinnamon stick
6 cloves
1/4 teaspoon cardamom seeds
2 teaspoons dried curry leaves
2 small dried red chilies

2 tablespoons vegetable oil
2 lbs. skinless, boneless chicken
  thighs, trimmed and cut in half
1 onion, chopped
2 cloves garlic, crushed
2 teaspoons finely grated fresh ginger
1 teaspoon ground turmeric
2 14-oz. cans whole peeled tomatoes
2/3 cup coconut milk
1/2 cup roasted cashews

Dry fry the coriander, cumin, and the fennel and fenugreek seeds separately over low heat until fragrant. Make sure the spices are well browned, but not burned. Place the seeds in a food processor or mortar and pestle, add the other ingredients, and grind to a powder.

Heat the oil in a large frying pan. Cook the chicken in batches for 10 minutes or until browned all over. Remove and drain on paper towels.

Drain all but 1 tablespoon of oil from the pan. Add the onion, garlic, ginger, and turmeric, and cook for 10 minutes or until the onion is soft. Add 2 tablespoons of the curry powder and cook, stirring, for 3 minutes or until fragrant.

Add the tomatoes and 1/2 teaspoon salt, bring to a boil, then reduce the heat and simmer. Return the chicken to the pan and stir until coated with the sauce. Simmer, covered, for 15 minutes, then uncovered for 15 minutes or until the chicken is tender and the sauce has thickened. Stir in the coconut milk and simmer for 3 minutes. Garnish with the cashews and serve with rice.

Serves 6

# Red curry of roast squash, beans, and basil

1¼ lbs. peeled and seeded butternut
   squash, cut into 1-inch cubes
2 tablespoons vegetable oil
1 tablespoon store-bought
   red curry paste
1²⁄₃ cups coconut cream (see Note)
1½ cups green beans, cut into
   1¼-inch pieces
2 kaffir lime leaves, crushed
1 tablespoon light brown sugar
1 tablespoon fish sauce
1 cup fresh Thai basil leaves, plus
   extra to garnish
1 tablespoon lime juice

Preheat the oven to 400°F. Place
the squash in a baking dish with
1 tablespoon oil and toss to coat.
Bake for 20 minutes or until tender.

Heat the remaining oil in a saucepan,
add the curry paste, and cook,
stirring constantly and breaking up
with a fork, over medium heat for
1–2 minutes. Add the coconut cream,
½ cup at a time, stirring with a
wooden spoon between each
addition for a creamy consistency.
Then add the squash and any
roasting juices, the beans, and kaffir
lime leaves. Reduce the heat to low
and cook for 5 minutes.

Stir in the brown sugar, fish sauce,
basil, and lime juice. Garnish with
extra basil leaves. Serve with rice.

Serves 4

Note: If you want to make this into
a lighter meal, use reduced-fat
coconut cream instead of the regular
version; the texture will be slightly
different, but the flavor of the curry
will still be good.

One pots

# Moroccan vegetable stew with minty couscous

2 tablespoons olive oil
1 onion, finely chopped
3 cloves garlic, finely chopped
1 teaspoon ground ginger
1 teaspoon ground turmeric
2 teaspoons ground cumin
2 teaspoons ground cinnamon
1/2 teaspoon dried chili flakes
13-oz. can diced tomatoes
13-oz. can chickpeas, rinsed and
  drained
1/2 cup golden raisins
3/4 lb. butternut squash, peeled
  and cut into 1-inch cubes
2 large zucchini, cut into
  3/4-inch pieces
2 carrots, cut into 3/4-inch pieces
1 cup instant couscous
1 tablespoon butter
4 tablespoons chopped fresh mint

Heat the olive oil in a large saucepan over medium heat. Add the onion and cook for 3–5 minutes or until translucent but not brown. Add the garlic, ginger, turmeric, cumin, cinnamon, and chili flakes, and cook for 1 minute. Add the tomatoes, chickpeas, golden raisins, and 1 cup water. Bring to a boil, then reduce the heat and simmer, covered, for 20 minutes. Add the squash, zucchini, and carrots, and cook for another 20 minutes or until the vegetables are tender. Season with salt and black pepper.

Place the couscous in a large heatproof bowl. Cover with 1 cup boiling water and allow to rest for 5 minutes or until all the water is absorbed. Fluff with a fork and stir in the butter and mint. Season with salt and ground black pepper and serve with the stew.

Serves 4

# Lamb tagine

1 tablespoon ground cumin
1 teaspoon ground ginger
1/2 teaspoon ground turmeric
1 teaspoon paprika
1/3 teaspoon ground cinnamon
2 cloves garlic, crushed
1/3 cup olive oil
3 lbs. diced lamb shoulder
2 onions, sliced
2 cups beef stock
2 tomatoes, peeled and chopped
1/2 teaspoon saffron threads
1 carrot, cut into matchsticks
1/2 cup chopped fresh cilantro leaves
1 cup pitted Kalamata olives
1 teaspoon preserved lemon zest,
   finely chopped and rinsed
   (see Note)
2 cups instant couscous
1/4 cup butter
1 1/2 tablespoons honey

Place the cumin, ginger, turmeric, paprika, cinnamon, crushed garlic, 2 tablespoons oil, and 1 teaspoon salt in a large bowl. Mix together, add the lamb, and toss to coat. Refrigerate for 2 hours.

Heat the remaining oil in a large saucepan over medium heat, add the lamb in batches, and cook for 5–6 minutes or until browned. Return the meat to the dish, add the onions, and cook for 1–2 minutes. Add the stock, tomatoes, saffron, carrot, and cilantro. Bring to a boil, then reduce the heat to low and cook, covered, for 1 hour. Add the olives and preserved lemon zest and cook, uncovered, for 30 minutes.

Place the couscous in a large heatproof bowl. Add 1 1/2 cups boiling water and allow to rest for 3–5 minutes. Stir in the butter and fluff up with a fork. Season. Spoon into deep bowls, top with the tagine, and drizzle with the honey.

Serves 4

Note: Only use the rinsed zest of preserved lemons. Discard the bitter pith and flesh.

## Italian beef casserole with polenta dumplings

2 tablespoons olive oil
1 onion, sliced
2 cloves garlic, crushed
1 tablespoon all-purpose flour
2 lbs. blade or chuck steak, cut into
  1-inch cubes
1½ cups beef stock
1 tablespoon chopped fresh oregano
2 14-oz. cans tomatoes
2 red peppers, roasted, peeled, and
  cut into strips
⅔ cup instant polenta
⅓ cup store-bought pesto

Preheat the oven to 300°F. Heat the oil in a 4-quart flameproof casserole dish, add the onion and garlic, and cook over medium heat for 8 minutes or until soft but not brown. Sprinkle the flour over the top and stir well. Add the beef, stock, oregano, tomatoes, and peppers, season and simmer for 15 minutes, then bake, covered, for 1½ hours.

Place 1¼ cups water in a saucepan, bring to a boil, then reduce the heat and simmer. Pour in the polenta in a thin stream, season, and cook, stirring, for 2 minutes or until it thickens and comes away from the side of the pan. Remove and cool.

Shape the cooled polenta into 12 round dumplings, place on top of the casserole, and bake, covered, for 1 hour, and then uncovered for 20–30 minutes. Garnish with the pesto and serve.

Serves 4–6

# Catalan fish stew

10 oz. boneless red mullet fillets
13 oz. boneless, firm white fish fillets
10 oz. calamari, cleaned
6 cups fish stock
⅓ cup olive oil
1 onion, chopped
6 cloves garlic, chopped
1 small fresh red chili, chopped
1 teaspoon paprika
pinch saffron threads
½ cup white wine
14-oz. can crushed tomatoes
16 medium shrimp, peeled, deveined,
   tails intact
2 tablespoons brandy
24 black mussels, cleaned
1 tablespoon chopped fresh parsley

*Picada*
2 tablespoons olive oil
2 slices day-old bread, cubed
2 cloves garlic
5 blanched almonds, toasted
2 tablespoons fresh Italian parsley

Cut the fish and calamari into
1½-inch pieces. Place the stock in a
large saucepan and bring to a boil for
15 minutes or until reduced by half.

To make the picada, heat the oil
in a frying pan and cook the bread,
stirring, for 2 minutes or until golden,
adding the garlic for the last minute.
Place all of the ingredients in a food
processor and process, adding stock
to make a smooth paste.

Heat 2 tablespoons of the oil in
a saucepan, add the onion, garlic,
chili, and paprika, and cook, stirring,
for 1 minute. Add the saffron, wine,
tomatoes, and stock. Bring to a boil,
then simmer. Heat the remaining oil
in a frying pan and fry the fish and
calamari for 3–5 minutes. Remove
from the frying pan. Add the shrimp,
cook for 1 minute, then pour in the
brandy. Carefully ignite the brandy
and let the flames burn down.
Remove from the frying pan.

Add the mussels to the pan and
simmer, covered, for 2–3 minutes or
until opened. Discard any that do not
open. Add all the seafood and the
picada to the frying pan, stirring until
the sauce has thickened and the
seafood is cooked. Season, sprinkle
with parsley, and serve.

Serves 6–8

# Mediterranean chicken stew

1 teaspoon ground cumin
1 teaspoon ground coriander
1 teaspoon paprika
1/4 teaspoon ground ginger
3 lbs. boneless chicken thighs,
    quartered
2 tablespoons olive oil
1 large onion, sliced
3 cloves garlic, finely chopped
2 teaspoons fresh oregano, chopped
1 cup dry white wine
14-oz. can crushed tomatoes
1 1/4 cups chicken stock
2 fresh bay leaves, crushed
1/4 teaspoon saffron threads, soaked
    in 2 tablespoons warm water
1/4 cup good-quality pitted green
    olives
1/4 cup good-quality pitted black
    olives
1/2 preserved lemon, flesh removed
    and zest cut into fine slivers
3 tablespoons finely chopped fresh
    Italian parsley
fresh basil sprigs, to garnish

Combine the cumin, coriander, paprika, and ginger, and rub over the chicken pieces.

Heat the oil in a large saucepan. Add the chicken in batches and cook over medium heat for 5 minutes or until browned. Remove from the saucepan.

Reduce the heat, add the onion, and cook, stirring constantly, for 5 minutes or until golden. Add the garlic and oregano and cook for 2 minutes, then add the wine and cook for 6 minutes or until nearly evaporated. Add the tomatoes, stock, bay leaves, saffron, and soaking liquid, and bring to a boil. Return the chicken to the saucepan and season well. Reduce the heat and simmer, covered, for 30 minutes or until the chicken is cooked through.

Stir in the olives and preserved lemon and cook, uncovered, for 10 minutes. Stir in the parsley, garnish with the sprigs of basil, and serve.

Serves 4–6

Note: This stew is delicious served with mashed potatoes. For extra flavor, stir some shredded fresh basil through the potatoes before serving.

## Osso buco with gremolata

1³/₄ lbs. veal shank (osso buco)
2 tablespoons olive oil
1 large carrot, finely chopped
1 large onion, finely chopped
3 cloves garlic, crushed
1 cup dry white wine
1 bay leaf, crumbled
2 14-oz. cans diced tomatoes
1¹/₂ cups chicken stock

*Gremolata*
1 clove garlic, finely chopped
2 tablespoons finely chopped fresh
  parsley
1 teaspoon finely grated lemon zest
1 anchovy fillet, rinsed and finely
  chopped

Preheat the oven to 300°F. Season the shanks. Heat the oil over medium heat in a flameproof casserole, add the shanks, and brown on all sides. Remove. Add the carrot, onion, and garlic, and cook for 3–5 minutes or until softened. Stir in the wine and bay leaf and cook for 5 minutes or until reduced by half. Return the shanks and add the tomatoes and stock. Bring to a boil. Cover, place in the oven, and bake, turning the meat occasionally, for 1³/₄–2 hours or until the meat is tender.

Remove the shanks and cool slightly. Remove the meat from the bones and chop coarsely. Push the marrow out of the bones and discard the bones. Return the meat and marrow to the tomato sauce and cook on the stovetop for 20 minutes or until reduced slightly. Season.

Combine the gremolata ingredients.

Divide the osso buco among four serving bowls and sprinkle with the gremolata. Serve with pasta.

Serves 4

# Chicken casserole with mustard and tarragon sauce

1/4 cup olive oil
2 lbs. boneless chicken thighs, halved, then quartered
1 onion, finely chopped
1 leek, sliced
1 clove garlic, finely chopped
3/4 lb. button mushrooms, sliced
1/2 teaspoon dried tarragon
1 1/2 cups chicken stock
3/4 cup cream
2 teaspoons lemon juice
2 teaspoons Dijon mustard

Preheat the oven to 350°F. Heat 1 tablespoon oil in a flameproof casserole over medium heat and cook the chicken in two batches for 6–7 minutes each or until golden. Remove from the dish and set aside.

Add the remaining oil to the dish and cook the onion, leek, and garlic over medium heat for 5 minutes or until soft. Add the mushrooms and cook for 5–7 minutes or until they are soft and browned, and most of the liquid has evaporated. Add the tarragon, chicken stock, cream, lemon juice, and mustard, bring to a boil, and cook for 2 minutes. Return the chicken pieces to the dish and season well. Cover.

Place the casserole in the oven and cook for 1 hour or until the sauce has reduced and thickened. Season to taste and serve with boiled new potatoes and a green salad.

Serves 4

## Tofu stroganoff

2 tablespoons all-purpose flour
1 tablespoon paprika
1 lb. firm tofu, cut into ½-inch cubes
1 tablespoon soybean oil
2 teaspoons tomato paste
¼ cup dry sherry
2 cups vegetable stock
12 pickled onions, halved
1 clove garlic, crushed
2½ cups field mushrooms, cut
   into ½-inch slices
3 tablespoons sour cream
sour cream, extra, to garnish
2 tablespoons chopped fresh
   chives

Combine the flour and paprika in a plastic bag and season well. Add the tofu and shake to coat.

Heat the oil in a frying pan. Add the tofu and cook over medium heat for 4 minutes or until golden. Add the tomato paste and cook for another minute. Add 2 tablespoons of the sherry, cook for 30 seconds, then transfer the tofu to a bowl. Keep any remaining flour in the pan.

Pour 1 cup of the stock into the pan and bring to a boil. Add the onions, garlic, and mushrooms, reduce the heat to medium, and simmer, covered, for 10 minutes. Return the tofu to the pan with the remaining sherry and stock. Season to taste. Return to a boil, reduce the heat, and simmer for 5 minutes or until heated through and the sauce has thickened.

Remove the pan from the heat and stir a little of the sauce into the sour cream until smooth and of pouring consistency; add to the pan. Garnish with a dollop of the extra sour cream and sprinkle with the chopped chives. Serve with noodles or steamed rice.

Serves 4

## Chili con carne

1 tablespoon olive oil
1 onion, chopped
3 cloves garlic, crushed
2 tablespoons ground cumin
1 1/2 teaspoons chili powder
1 1/4 lbs. ground beef
14-oz. can crushed tomatoes
2 tablespoons tomato paste
2 teaspoons dried oregano
1 teaspoon dried thyme
2 cups beef stock
1 teaspoon sugar
10 oz. canned red kidney beans,
    rinsed and drained
1 cup grated cheddar
1/2 cup sour cream
2 tablespoons finely chopped
    fresh cilantro leaves
corn chips, to serve

Heat the oil in a large saucepan over medium heat, add the onion, and cook for 5 minutes or until starting to brown. Add the garlic, cumin, chili powder, and ground beef, and cook, stirring, for 5 minutes or until the beef has changed color. Break up any lumps with the back of a wooden spoon. Add the tomatoes, tomato paste, herbs, beef stock, and sugar, and stir to combine. Reduce the heat to low and cook, stirring occasionally, for 1 hour or until the sauce is rich and thick. Stir in the beans and cook for 2 minutes to heat through.

Divide the chili con carne among 6 serving bowls, sprinkle with the cheese, and top with a tablespoon of sour cream. Garnish with the cilantro. Serve with corn chips or rice.

Serves 6

# Bean and pepper stew

1 cup dried kidney beans
  (see Note)
2 tablespoons olive oil
2 large cloves garlic, crushed
1 red onion, halved and cut into
  thin wedges
1 red pepper, cut into 1/2-inch cubes
1 green pepper, cut into 1/2-inch
  cubes
2 14-oz. cans diced tomatoes
2 tablespoons tomato paste
2 cups vegetable stock
2 tablespoons chopped fresh basil
2/3 cup Kalamata olives, pitted
1–2 teaspoons light brown sugar

Put the beans in a large bowl, cover with cold water, and soak overnight. Rinse well, then transfer to a large saucepan, cover with cold water, and cook for 45 minutes or until just tender. Drain.

Heat the oil in a large saucepan. Cook the garlic and onion over medium heat for 2–3 minutes or until the onion is soft. Add the red and green peppers and cook for another 5 minutes.

Stir in the tomatoes, tomato paste, stock, and beans. Simmer, covered, for 40 minutes or until the beans are cooked through. Stir in the basil, olives, and sugar. Season with salt and black pepper. Serve hot with crusty bread.

Serves 4–6

Note: 1 cup of dried kidney beans yields about 2 1/2 cups cooked beans. You can use 2 1/2 cups canned kidney or borlotti beans instead if you prefer.

# Spicy sausage stew

2 tablespoons olive oil
1 1/2 lbs. Italian sausage, cut into
  1 1/2-inch pieces
1 leek, finely sliced
1 red pepper, seeded and chopped
14-oz. can diced tomatoes
1/2 cup chicken stock
1 1/4 cups canned butter beans,
  rinsed and drained
1 1/3 cups instant couscous
1 tablespoon butter, melted
2 tablespoons fresh Italian parsley

Heat half the oil in a saucepan over medium heat, add the sausage, and cook for 6 minutes or until browned. Remove. Cook the sliced leek in the remaining oil over low heat for 10–12 minutes or until soft. Add the pepper and cook for 1–2 minutes. Return the sausage to the saucepan and stir in the tomatoes and stock. Bring to a boil, then reduce the heat and simmer for 30 minutes. Add the beans, season, and stir for 1–2 minutes to heat through.

Place the couscous in a heatproof bowl with 1 1/3 cups boiling water and a pinch of salt. Leave for 5 minutes, fluff up, and stir in the butter. Divide among 4 bowls and spoon on the stew. Garnish with the parsley.

Serves 4

# Greek octopus in red wine stew

2-lb. baby octopus
2 tablespoons olive oil
1 large onion, chopped
3 cloves garlic, crushed
1 bay leaf
3 cups red wine
1/4 cup red wine vinegar
14-oz. can crushed tomatoes
1 tablespoon tomato paste
1 tablespoon chopped fresh oregano
1/4 teaspoon ground cinnamon
small pinch ground cloves
1 teaspoon sugar
2 tablespoons finely chopped fresh
   Italian parsley

Cut between the head and tentacles of the octopus, just below the eyes. Grasp the body and push the beak out and up through the center of the tentacles with your fingers. Cut the eyes from the head by slicing a small round off. Discard the eye section. Carefully slit through one side, avoiding the ink sac, and remove the gut from inside. Rinse the octopus well under running water.

Heat the oil in a large saucepan, add the onion, and cook over medium heat for 5 minutes or until starting to brown. Add the garlic and bay leaf and cook for another minute. Add the octopus and stir to coat in the onion mixture.

Stir in the wine, vinegar, tomatoes, tomato paste, oregano, cinnamon, cloves, and sugar. Bring to a boil, then reduce the heat and simmer for 1 hour or until the octopus is tender and the sauce has thickened slightly. Stir in the parsley and season to taste with salt and ground black pepper. Serve with a Greek salad and crusty bread to mop up the delicious juices.

Serves 4–6

# Asian-flavored beef stew

2 tablespoons olive oil
2 lbs. chuck steak, cut into
  1-inch cubes
1 large red onion, thickly sliced
3 cloves garlic, crushed
3 tablespoons tomato paste
1 cup red wine
2 cups beef stock
2 bay leaves, crushed
3 strips orange zest, ½ inch long
1 star anise
1 teaspoon Szechuan peppercorns
1 teaspoon chopped fresh thyme
1 tablespoon chopped fresh
  rosemary
3 tablespoons chopped fresh
  cilantro leaves

Heat 1 tablespoon oil in a large
saucepan, add the beef, and cook
in batches over medium heat for
2 minutes or until browned. Remove.

Heat the remaining oil, add the onion
and garlic, and cook for 5 minutes.
Add the tomato paste, cook for
3 minutes, then stir in the wine
and cook for 2 minutes.

Return the meat to the saucepan
and add the stock, bay leaves,
orange zest, star anise, Szechuan
peppercorns, thyme, and rosemary.
Reduce the heat to low and simmer,
covered, for 1½–2 hours or until
tender. Remove the bay leaves and
zest. Stir in 2½ tablespoons cilantro
and garnish with the remainder. Serve
with rice.

Serves 4

# Chinese beef in soy

1 1/2 lbs. chuck steak, trimmed and
  cut into 1-inch cubes
1/3 cup dark soy sauce
2 tablespoons honey
1 tablespoon rice vinegar
3 tablespoons soybean oil
4 cloves garlic, chopped
8 scallions, finely sliced
1 tablespoon finely grated fresh
  ginger
2 star anise
1/2 teaspoon ground cloves
1 1/2 cups beef stock
1/2 cup red wine
scallions, extra, sliced,
  to garnish

Place the meat in a nonmetallic dish.
Combine the soy sauce, honey, and
vinegar in a small bowl, then pour
over the meat. Cover with plastic
wrap and marinate for at least
2 hours—preferably overnight.
Drain, setting aside the marinade,
and pat the cubes dry.

Place 1 tablespoon of the oil in
a saucepan and brown the meat
in 3 batches, for 3–4 minutes per
batch—add another tablespoon
of oil, if necessary. Remove the
meat. Add the remaining oil and fry
the garlic, scallions, ginger, star
anise, and cloves for 1–2 minutes
or until fragrant.

Return all the meat to the saucepan,
add the marinade, stock, and wine.
Bring the liquid to a boil and simmer,
covered, for 1 hour, 15 minutes.
Cook, uncovered, for 15 minutes or
until the sauce is syrupy and the
meat is tender.

Garnish with the sliced scallions and
serve immediately with steamed rice.

Serves 4

# Mushroom ragu with polenta

1/4 oz. dried porcini mushrooms
1 tablespoon butter
1 tablespoon olive oil
4 cloves garlic, finely chopped
3/4 lb. mixed mushrooms (shiitake, cap, portobello), sliced if large
1 cup red wine
2 cups beef stock
3 tablespoons finely chopped fresh parsley
2 teaspoons chopped fresh thyme
1 cup enoki mushrooms
1 cup polenta
2 tablespoons butter
1/3 cup grated Parmesan

Soak the porcini in 3/4 cup warm water for 15 minutes. Drain and chop, saving the soaking liquid.

Heat the butter and oil in a saucepan, add the garlic, and cook over medium heat for 3 minutes. Add the mixed mushrooms and cook for 3 minutes. Stir in the red wine and cook for 5 minutes. Add the porcini, soaking liquid, stock, and parsley. Cook over medium heat for 25 minutes or until the liquid has reduced by half. Stir in the thyme and enoki, and keep warm.

Bring 4 cups lightly salted water to a boil in a large saucepan, then reduce the heat to medium. Stir with a wooden spoon to form a whirlpool and add the polenta in a very thin stream. Cook, stirring, for 20 minutes or until the polenta comes away from the side of the saucepan. Stir in the butter and Parmesan, and serve immediately with the ragu on top.

Serves 4

# Boston baked soybeans

1 lb. dried soybeans
2 onions, chopped
1 tablespoon molasses
1/4 cup turbinado (raw) sugar
3 teaspoons dried mustard
2 smoked pork hocks
 (about 1 1/4 lbs. each)
2 tablespoons tomato sauce

Soak the soybeans in a large bowl of cold water for at least 8 hours—preferably overnight. Drain. Place in a large saucepan and cover with fresh water. Bring to a boil and simmer for 2 hours, topping up with water if necessary. Drain and set aside 2 cups of the cooking liquid.

Preheat the oven to 315°F. Place the cooking liquid in a 4-quart heavy-bottomed, flameproof casserole. Add the onion, molasses, turbinado sugar, mustard, and 1/2 teaspoon black pepper. Bring slowly to a boil. Reduce the heat and simmer for 2 minutes.

Add the beans and pork hocks. Bake, covered, for 3 hours, stirring once or twice during cooking—add a little water, if necessary, to keep the beans covered with liquid. Stir in the tomato sauce and bake, uncovered, for another 30 minutes.

Remove the meat and skim any fat off the surface of the beans. Roughly shred the meat and return to the bean mixture. Serve hot.

Serves 4–6

## Irish beef hotpot

2 lbs. chuck steak, cut into
  1-inch cubes
seasoned flour, to coat
2 tablespoons olive oil
2 large onions, sliced
2 cloves garlic, crushed
2 bay leaves
2 teaspoons chopped fresh thyme
1 tablespoon chopped fresh parsley
1½ cups beef stock
4 potatoes, cut into 1-inch cubes
2 carrots, cut into ¾-inch pieces

Preheat the oven to 325°F. Toss the meat in the seasoned flour to coat. Heat the oil in a frying pan over medium heat, add the beef in batches, and cook for 4–5 minutes or until browned. Drain and place in a 4-quart flameproof casserole.

Add the onion and garlic to the frying pan and cook for 5 minutes or until softened and lightly golden. Add the bay leaves, thyme, and half the parsley, stirring, then pour in the stock, stirring to remove any sediment stuck to the bottom or side of the pan. Transfer the stock mixture to the casserole, cover, and bake for 1½ hours.

Add the potatoes and carrots to the casserole, and add a little water if necessary. Return to the oven and cook for 1 hour or until the meat and vegetables are tender. Garnish with the remaining parsley.

Serves 4

Note: This dish is delicious if made a day ahead and gently reheated.

## Spanish-style chicken casserole

2 tablespoons light olive oil
1½ lbs. chicken thighs
1½ lbs. chicken drumsticks
1 large onion, chopped
2 cloves garlic, crushed
2 teaspoons sweet paprika
1 large red pepper, sliced
¾ cup dry sherry
14-oz. can peeled tomatoes
2 tablespoons tomato paste
¾ cup green olives, pitted and halved
1 teaspoon sweet paprika, extra

Preheat the oven to 350°F. Heat the oil in a large frying pan, add the chicken in batches, and cook over medium heat for 3–4 minutes or until browned. Transfer to a 4-quart flameproof casserole. Add the onion, garlic, paprika, and pepper to the frying pan and cook for 5–8 minutes or until softened. Add the sherry and cook for 2 minutes or until slightly reduced. Add the tomatoes and tomato paste, stir well, and cook for 2 minutes. Pour the tomato mixture over the chicken and add 1 cup water.

Bake, covered, for 1 hour, 15 minutes, then uncovered for 15 minutes. Add the olives and leave for 10 minutes. Garnish with the extra paprika and serve with rice.

Serves 4

# Spicy vegetable stew with dhal

*Dhal*
3/4 cup yellow split peas
2-inch piece fresh ginger, grated
2–3 cloves garlic, crushed
1 fresh red chili, seeded and
   chopped

3 tomatoes
2 tablespoons oil
1 teaspoon yellow mustard seeds
1 teaspoon cumin seeds
1 teaspoon ground cumin
1/2 teaspoon garam masala
1 red onion, cut into thin wedges
3 slender eggplants, cut into
   1-inch slices
2 carrots, cut into 1-inch slices
1/4 cauliflower, cut into florets
1 1/2 cups vegetable stock
2 small zucchini, cut into 1-inch slices
1/2 cup frozen peas
1/2 cup fresh cilantro leaves

To make the dhal, place the split peas in a bowl, cover with water, and soak for 2 hours. Drain. Place in a large saucepan with the ginger, garlic, chili, and 3 cups water. Bring to a boil, then reduce the heat and simmer for 45 minutes or until soft. Allow to cool slightly, then place in the bowl of a food processor or blender and process to a purée.

Score a cross in the bottom of the tomatoes, soak in boiling water for 2 minutes, then plunge into cold water and peel the skin away from the cross. Remove the seeds and roughly chop.

Heat the oil in a large saucepan. Cook the spices over medium heat for 30 seconds or until fragrant. Add the onion and cook for another 2 minutes or until the onion is soft. Stir in the tomatoes, eggplant, carrots, and cauliflower.

Add the dhal purée and stock, mix together well, and simmer, covered, for 45 minutes or until the vegetables are tender. Stir occasionally. Add the zucchini and peas during the last 10 minutes of cooking. Stir in the cilantro leaves and serve hot.

Serves 4–6

# Beef bourguignonne

2 lbs. chuck steak, cut into
  1-inch cubes
seasoned flour, to coat
2 tablespoons oil
7 oz. bacon, chopped
1½ tablespoons butter
¼ lb. pickled onions
3 cloves garlic, finely chopped
1 leek, sliced
3 cups button mushrooms
2 carrots, diced
3 tablespoons tomato paste
2 cups red wine
2 cups beef stock
2 teaspoons chopped fresh thyme
2 bay leaves
4 tablespoons finely chopped fresh
  Italian parsley

Toss the meat in the flour to coat. Shake off any excess. Heat the oil in a large saucepan, add the bacon, and cook over medium heat for 3–4 minutes or until lightly browned. Remove from the saucepan. Add the beef in small batches and cook for 3–4 minutes or until starting to brown. Remove from the saucepan.

Melt the butter in the saucepan, add the onions, garlic, and leek, and cook for 4–5 minutes or until softened.

Return the beef and bacon to the saucepan, add the remaining ingredients, except the parsley, and stir well. Bring to a boil, then reduce the heat and simmer, covered, stirring occasionally, for 1 hour, then uncovered for 30 minutes or until the meat is very tender and the sauce thickened. Remove the bay leaves and stir in the parsley. Serve with mashed potatoes.

Serves 6

# Pork and white bean chili

2³/₄ lbs. boneless pork shoulder, boned, trimmed, and cut into 1-inch cubes (1¹/₃–1³/₄ lbs. meat)
2–3 tablespoons vegetable oil
1 large onion, diced
3 cloves garlic, finely chopped
1 tablespoon sweet paprika
¹/₂ teaspoon chili powder
2 canned chipotle peppers or jalapeño chilies, chopped
1 tablespoon ground cumin
14-oz. can diced tomatoes
2 14-oz. cans cannellini beans, rinsed and drained
1 cup fresh cilantro leaves, coarsely chopped
sour cream, to serve
lime wedges, to serve

Season the pork. Heat 2 tablespoons oil in a large saucepan over high heat. Add half the pork and cook for 5 minutes or until brown. Remove. Repeat with the remaining pork, using more oil if necessary.

Lower the heat to medium, add the onion and garlic, and cook for 3–5 minutes or until soft. Add the paprika, chili powder, chipotle peppers, and cumin, and cook for 1 minute.

Return the pork to the saucepan. Add the tomatoes and 3 cups water and simmer, partially covered, for 1–1¹/₂ hours or until the pork is very tender. Add the beans and heat through. Boil a little longer to reduce the liquid, if necessary. Stir in the cilantro and season. Serve with sour cream and lime wedges.

Serves 4

## Tamarind beef

2 tablespoons oil
2 lbs. chuck steak, cut into
   1½-inch cubes
2 red onions, sliced
3 cloves garlic, finely chopped
1 tablespoon fresh ginger, julienned
2 teaspoons ground coriander
2 teaspoons ground cumin
½ teaspoon ground fenugreek seeds
½ teaspoon chili powder
½ teaspoon ground cloves
1 cinnamon stick
½ cup tamarind purée
6 fresh curry leaves
1 cup coconut cream
¾ cup green beans, halved
fresh cilantro sprigs, to garnish

Heat the oil in a large saucepan, add the beef in batches, and cook over high heat for 2–3 minutes or until browned. Remove.

Add the onion and cook over medium heat for 3 minutes or until soft, then add the garlic and ginger and cook for another 2 minutes. Add the coriander, cumin, fenugreek, chili powder, cloves, and cinnamon stick, and cook for 2 minutes.

Return the meat to the saucepan and stir to coat with the spices. Add the tamarind purée, curry leaves, and 1½ cups water. Bring to a boil, then reduce the heat and simmer, covered, for 1½ hours or until the beef is tender. Add the coconut cream and cook, uncovered, for another 10 minutes, then add the beans and cook for 5 minutes or until tender but still crisp. Garnish with the cilantro sprigs and serve with rice.

Serves 4

## Cypriot pork and coriander stew

1 ½ tablespoons coriander seeds
1 ¾ lbs. pork fillet, cut into
  1-inch cubes
1 tablespoon all-purpose flour
¼ cup olive oil
1 large onion, thinly sliced
1 ½ cups red wine
1 cup chicken stock
1 teaspoon sugar
fresh cilantro sprigs, to garnish

Crush the coriander seeds in a mortar and pestle. Combine the pork, crushed seeds, and ½ teaspoon cracked pepper in a bowl. Cover and marinate overnight in the refrigerator.

Combine the flour and pork and toss. Heat 2 tablespoons oil in a frying pan and cook the pork in batches over high heat for 1–2 minutes or until brown. Remove.

Heat the remaining oil, add the onion, and cook over medium heat for 2–3 minutes or until just golden. Return the meat to the pan, add the wine, stock, and sugar, and season. Bring to a boil, then reduce the heat and simmer, covered, for 1 hour.

Remove the meat. Return the pan to the heat and boil over high heat for 3–5 minutes or until reduced and slightly thickened. Pour over the meat and top with the cilantro sprigs.

Serves 4–6

# Goulash

4 oz. bacon, julienned
1 onion, chopped
2 tomatoes, peeled and chopped
1 clove garlic, chopped
1/2 teaspoon caraway seeds,
  lightly crushed
1 1/2 tablespoons sweet paprika
2 lbs. lamb fillet, trimmed and cut
  into 1-inch pieces
1 bay leaf
1 cup vegetable stock
1 lb. new potatoes, cut into
  1-inch pieces
2/3 cup fresh or frozen peas
3 tablespoons sour cream
sweet paprika, extra, to garnish

Place the bacon in a saucepan and cook over medium heat for 4–5 minutes. Add the onion and cook for 2 minutes, then add the tomatoes and cook for 1 minute.

Stir in the garlic, caraway seeds, paprika, lamb, bay leaf, and stock. Bring to a boil, then reduce the heat to low and simmer, covered, for 40 minutes.

Add the potatoes and cook, uncovered, for 15 minutes or until tender, then add the peas and cook for 5 minutes or until tender. Stir in the sour cream and gently heat, without boiling. Garnish with paprika and serve with rye bread.

Serves 6

## Chicken fricasee

1 tablespoon butter
1 tablespoon olive oil
2 cups button mushrooms, sliced
3 lbs. chicken pieces
1 onion, chopped
2 celery stalks, sliced
1 cup dry white wine
1 cup chicken stock
1 fresh bay leaf
1 cup whipping cream
2 lbs. russet potatoes, peeled
   and chopped
2/3 cup milk, heated
1/3 cup butter, extra
2 tablespoons chopped fresh parsley

Heat half the butter and oil in a large saucepan. Add the mushrooms and cook over medium heat for 5 minutes or until soft and golden. Remove from the saucepan with a slotted spoon. Heat the remaining oil and butter, add the chicken pieces in batches, and cook for 4 minutes or until browned. Remove from the saucepan.

Add the onion and celery to the saucepan and cook for 8 minutes or until soft. Pour in the white wine and stir well. Add the stock, chicken, mushrooms, bay leaf, and cream. Bring to a boil, then reduce the heat and simmer, covered, for 30–45 minutes or until the chicken is cooked through and tender.

Meanwhile, bring a large saucepan of water to a boil, add the potatoes, and cook for 10 minutes or until tender. Drain, add the milk and extra butter, and mash with a potato masher until smooth. Season with salt and freshly ground black pepper.

Add the chopped parsley to the chicken and season. Serve with mashed potatoes.

Serves 4

# Index

Angel-hair pasta with garlic, scallops, and
    arugula, 130
Asian barley pilaf, 213
Asian-flavored beef stew, 369
Asian salmon and noodle salad, 118
Asparagus and pistachio risotto, 197

Baked shrimp risotto with Thai flavors, 230
bean
    Boston baked soybeans, 374
    and pepper stew, 362
beef
    and beet borscht, 17
    bourguignonne, 382
    hotpot, Irish, 377
    pho, 45
    rendang, 334
Boston baked soybeans, 374
Braised vegetables with cashews, 287
Braised water spinach with tofu, 251
Bucatini with sausage and fennel seed, 166
Butter chicken, 297

Cajun scallops, conchigliette, and buttery
    corn sauce, 149
Caramelized onion and parsnip soup, 21
Catalan fish stew, 350
Cauliflower soup with smoked salmon
    croutons, 62
Cavatelli with pecorino and an herb sauce,
    145
Chiang mai noodles, 283
chicken
    and asparagus risotto, 221
    braised with ginger and star anise, 279
    Butter, 297
    casserole with mustard and tarragon
        sauce, 357
    and coconut soup, Thai-style, 22
    curry with apricots, 329

    fricasée, 393
    and galangal soup, 57
    gumbo, 198
    and mushroom pilaf, 201
    and mushroom risotto, 194
    and pork paella, 210
    and squash laksa, 34
    with Thai basil, chili, and cashews, 236
    Waldorf salad, 125
Chickpea curry, 317
Chickpea and flatbread salad, 97
Chickpea soup, 37
Chili beef, 288
Chili con carne, 361
Chinese beef and broccoli stir-fry, 259
Chinese beef in soy, 370
Chinese fried rice, 225
Corn and lemongrass soup with crayfish,
    46
Crab and corn eggflower noodle broth, 38
Crab and spinach soba noodle salad, 89
Creamy chicken and peppercorn
    pappardelle, 129
Creamy pasta gnocchi with peas and
    prosciutto, 141
Creamy pesto chicken penne, 173
Cresti di gallo with creamy tomato and bacon
    sauce, 182
Curried chicken noodle soup, 65
curry
    Chickpea, 317
    Goan pork, 305
    Green chicken, 318
    Light red seafood, 330
    Madras beef, 301
    Malaysian Nonya chicken, 310
    Musaman beef, 293
    Quick duck, 306
    Yellow fish, 314
Cypriot pork and coriander stew, 389

duck and noodle salad, Roast, 98
duck, Rice noodle soup with, 25
duck and somen noodle soup, Five-spice, 14

Family beef stir-fry, 243
Fattoush, 78
Fettucine with creamy spinach and roasted
    tomatoes, 158
Fish ball curry, 321
Five-spice duck and somen noodle soup,
    14
Fresh beet and goat cheese salad, 86
Fresh tuna Niçoise, 73
Fried noodles with chicken, pork, and
    shrimp, 271

Goan pork curry, 305
Goulash, 390
Greek octopus in red wine stew, 366
Greek salad, 117
Green chicken curry, 318
Green papaya salad, 85
Green pilaf with cashews, 206
Green tea noodle soup, 49
Grilled baby octopus salad, 110
Ground chicken salad, 248

Hearty bean and pasta soup, 26
Hot and sour shrimp soup, 41

Indian-style butter shrimp, 322
Irish beef hotpot, 377
Italian beef casserole with polenta
    dumplings, 349

Jambalaya, 229
Japanese pork and noodle stir-fry, 240

kofta, Lamb, 313
korma, Lamb, 326

lamb
    with hokkien noodles and sour sauce,
        264
    kofta, 313
    korma, 326
    and rice noodle salad with peanut
        dressing, 109
    tagine, 346
Lemon and zucchini risotto, 209
lentil pilaf, Rice and red, 222
lentil sauce, Penne with rustic, 157
Lentil and Swiss chard soup, 58
Light red seafood curry, 330
Linguine with ham, artichoke, and lemon
    sauce, 162

Macaroni & cheese with pancetta, 133
Madras beef curry, 301
Malaysian hot and sour pineapple curry,
    337
Malaysian Nonya chicken curry, 310
Mediterranean chicken stew, 253
Mee Grob, 275
Minestrone, 50
Miso soup with chicken and udon noodles,
    10
Moroccan vegetable stew with minty
    couscous, 345
Musaman beef curry, 293
mushroom
    ragu with polenta, 373
    risotto, 218

Niçoise, Fresh tuna, 73
Nonya chicken curry, Malaysian, 310
Noodle with beef, 267

Orange sweet potato and fried noodle salad,
    74
Osso buco with gremolata, 354

Paella, 202
paella, Chicken and pork, 210
Panang beef, 309
Paneer and pea curry, 333
pasta
  with baby spinach, squash, and
    tomatoes, 174
  with garlic, scallops and arugula, Angel
    hair, 130
  gnocchi with peas and prosciutto,
    Creamy, 141
  with gremolata, Osso buco, 354
  Prawn ricotta and spinach, 154
  with seared shrimp, 134
  soup, Hearty bean and, 26
  Tuna, tomato and rocket, 106
papaya salad, Green, 85
Pea and arugula soup, 30
Pea and ham soup, 54
Pear and walnut salad with lime vinaigrette,
  121
Penne with rustic lentil sauce, 157
Peppered pork, zucchini, and garganelli, 137
Phad Thai, 239
pork
  asparagus and baby corn stir-fry, 276
  and brown bean noodles, 244
  and glass noodle soup, 61
  and mushroom with white pepper, 263
  with plum sauce and choy sum, 280
  roast, 69
  shrimp and vermicelli salad in lettuce
    cups, 94

Quick duck curry, 306

Ramen noodle soup with roast pork and
  greens, 69
Red curry of roast squash, beans, and basil,
  341

Rice noodle soup with duck, 25
Rice and red lentil pilaf, 222
Risi e bisi, 193
Risotto with scallops and minted peas, 205
Roast duck and noodle salad, 98
Roast squash, feta, and arugula penne, 142
Roast squash sauce on pappardelle, 185
Roasted fennel and orange salad, 93
Roasted tomatoes and ricotta tagliatelle, 161
Rogan josh, 294
Rotelle with chickpeas, tomatoes, and
  parsley, 150

Salmon and potato salad, 77
Seafood soup with rouille, 66
shrimp
  laksa, 18
  pilaf, 217
  potato and corn chowder, 29
  prosciutto and arugula salad, 113
  ricotta and spinach pasta, 154
  and saffron potato salad, 90
  salad with Asian dressing, 102
  and snow pea stir-fry, 272
  tomato and saffron pasta, 169
  and udon noodle salad with lime dressing,
    105
  and white bean chili, 385
Singapore noodles, 260
Smoked trout Caesar salad, 101
Spaghetti Bolognese, 181
Spaghetti marinara, 153
Spaghetti with olive, caper, and anchovy
  sauce, 138
Spaghetti with smoked tuna and olives, 189
Spaghettini with herbs, baby spinach, and
  garlic crumbs, 170
Spanish-style chicken casserole, 378
Spicy eggplant stir-fry, 268
Spicy squash and coconut soup, 9

Spicy sausage stew, 365
Spicy vegetable stew with dhal, 381
Squash risotto, 214
Squid salad, 82
Sri Lankan chicken curry with cashews, 338
Stir-fried lamb with mint and chilies, 247
Stir-fried scallops with sugar snap peas, 256
Sukiyaki soup, 53
Sweet chili shrimp, 235
Sweet pork, 255
sweet potato and fried noodle salad,
    Orange, 74
Sweet potato gnocchi with wilted greens,
    178
Sweet potato and pear soup, 42
Sweet potato and sage risotto, 226

Tagliatelle with chicken, herbs, and
    mushrooms, 186
Tamarind beef, 386
Thai beef and squash curry, 325
Thai beef salad, 114
Thai jungle curry shrimp, 302
Thai-style chicken and coconut soup, 22
Tofu stroganoff, 358

Tomato bread soup, 13
Tortellini boscaiola, 146
Tuna, tomato, and arugula pasta salad, 106

Veal tortellini with creamy mushroom sauce,
    177
Vegetable ramen, 33
Vegetable and tofu puff stir-fry with
    barbecued pork, 284
Vietnamese chicken salad, 81
Vietnamese shrimp and cabbage salad, 122

Waldorf salad, Chicken, 125
walnut salad with lime vinaigrette, Pear and,
    121
water spinach with tofu, Braised, 251
Wonton chicken ravioli with a Thai dressing,
    165

Yakiudon, 252
Yellow curry with vegetables, 298
Yellow fish curry, 314

zucchini and garganelli, Peppered pork, 137
zucchini risotto, Lemon and, 209

*Photographers:* Cris Cordeiro, Craig Cranko, Joe Filshie, Roberto Jean François, Ian Hofstetter, Andre Martin, Rob Reichenfeld, Brett Stevens

*Food Stylists:* Marie-Hélène Clauzon, Jane Collins, Sarah de Nardi, Georgina Dolling, Cherise Koch, Michelle Noerianto

*Food Preparation:* Alison Adams, Justine Johnson, Valli Little, Ben Masters, Kate Murdoch, Kim Passenger, Justine Poole, Christine Sheppard, Angela Tregonning

**Laurel Glen Publishing**
An imprint of the Advantage Publishers Group
5880 Oberlin Drive, San Diego, CA 92121-4794
www.advantagebooksonline.com

All notations of errors or omissions should be addressed to Laurel Glen Publishing,
editorial department, at the above address. All other correspondence (author inquiries,
permissions and rights) concerning the content of this book should be addressed to
Murdoch Books, GPO Box 1203, Sydney NSW, 1045, Australia.

ISBN 1-57145-831-X

Library of Congress Cataloging-in-Publication Data available upon request.

Printed by Tien Wah Press, Singapore.

2 3 4 5 06 05 04 03 02

Editorial Director: Diana Hill. Managing Editor: Rachel Carter. Series Editor: Katharine Gasparini.
U.S. Editor: Kerry MacKenzie Creative Director: Marylouise Brammer. Designer: Michelle Cutler
Food Director: Jane Lawson
Photographer (chapter openers): Ian Hofstetter. Stylist (chapter openers): Cherise Koch
Picture Librarian: Genevieve Huard

Chief Executive: Juliet Rogers
Publisher: Kay Scarlett
Production Manager: Kylie Kirkwood

NOTE: Those who might be at risk from the effects of salmonella poisoning (the elderly, pregnant women,
young children, and those suffering from immune deficiency diseases) should consult their doctor with
any concerns about eating raw eggs.

Front cover: Shrimp laksa, page 18
Back cover: Chicken Waldorf salad, page 125